STUDIES IN THE BOOK OF JOB

A BIBLICAL DRAMA

STUDIES IN THE BOOK OF JOB

*A BIBLICAL DRAMA ILLUMINATING THE
PROBLEM OF THE AGES*

FOR ADVANCED CLASSES IN THE SUNDAY SCHOOL, FOR BIBLICAL
LITERATURE COURSES IN HIGH SCHOOLS AND COLLEGES,
FOR EVENING SERVICES, AND FOR INDIVIDUAL USE

BY

REV. FRANCIS N. PELOUBET, D.D.

Author of "Select Notes on the International Lessons,"
"The Teacher's Commentary on Acts," etc.

WIPF & STOCK · Eugene, Oregon

Wipf and Stock Publishers
199 W 8th Ave, Suite 3
Eugene, OR 97401

Studies in the Book of Job
A Biblical Drama Illuminating the Problem of the Ages
By Peloubet, Francis N.
ISBN 13: 978-1-62564-381-0
Publication date 10/1/2013
Previously published by Scribner, 1906

GENERAL PLAN

READINGS IN CHARACTER.   A FULL BIBLIOGRAPHY.

REFERENCES FOR BIBLE STUDY.

BLACKBOARD DIAGRAMS.

SUGGESTIVE ILLUSTRATIONS AND APPLICATIONS.

TOPICS FOR RESEARCH AND DISCUSSION.

BRIEF NOTES ON DIFFICULT AND STRIKING PASSAGES.

POINTS OF CONTACT WITH DAILY LIFE, LITERATURE,
AND HISTORY—SCHOLARLY, SPIRITUAL,
EDUCATIONAL, DEVOTIONAL.

" This is the cry
   That echoes through the wilderness of earth,
   Through song and sorrow, day of death and birth:
   'WHY?'

" It is the high
   Wail of the child with all his life to face,
   Man's last dumb question as he reaches space:
   'WHY?'"

PREFACE

THE lessons in this book and the method of presenting the subject have grown out of actual experience. It has been tested in the class room and found to create a deep interest, to meet the needs of many souls, and to give a new vision of its beauty and power.

I am led the more earnestly to commend the study of the Book of Job, because its subject has to do with all classes and conditions of men, and because of my own experience in connection with it. I had, of course, read it many times, but during my earlier ministry I sympathized with Macaulay's words concerning Milton's "Paradise Lost" as applying equally to the Book of Job, that it was "the most admired and least read of all poems," and I did not understand how such men as Tennyson and Daniel Webster could regard it as "the greatest poem in all literature."

But a combination of circumstances led to a study of the book which opened my eyes to its wonderful poetic structure, its dramatic situations, its bursts of eloquence, its literary gems, its spiritual insight, its use of every known poetic form.

> "Then felt I like some watcher of the sky
> When a new planet swims into his ken."

So that it is easy to accept Carlyle's dictum, in his "Hero as Prophet," that the Book of Job is "one of the grandest things ever written with pen. . . . There is nothing written, I think, in the Bible or out of it, of equal literary merit." Professor Moulton, in his introduction to Job in his "Modern Reader's Bible" expresses this opinion: "If a jury of persons well instructed in literature were impanelled to pronounce upon the question, 'What is the greatest poem in the world's great literatures,' while on such a question unanimity would be impossible, yet I believe a large majority would give their verdict in favor of . . . the Book of Job." Froude looks forward to the day "when, perhaps, the Book of Job will be seen towering up alone far above all the poetry of the world."

The critical questions concerning the book—its age, date, author or authors, method of composition or growth, later additions versus unity, place in the religious history of Israel—have not been neglected. Abundant references have been given where these discussions may be found by all who wish to make a thorough study of them. But the main emphasis has been placed on the book as it is now, on the inspiring, invigorating, transforming, comforting teachings found therein. It is not the history of the violin we here want, but the music.

The aim is to enable the members of an ordinary class to receive the full impression the Book of Job was written to produce:

To awaken fresh interest in the book itself.

To open doors to its greatness and glory as literature.

To open windows to its blessed and comforting truths.

To bring its consolations to the perplexed and suffering.

To apply its character-forming elements and power.

CONTENTS

FOREWORD TO TEACHERS

THE Book of Job lends itself to every form of teaching, whether by lecture or question and answer or formal reports or mutual investigation and conversation. There is no best way for all teachers and all classes. The same teacher can often wisely use more than one method. Some form of question and answer is usually most effective; but do not be misled by those who say that "lecturing is not teaching," provided you can lecture so interestingly as to set your scholars to thinking. Most of the education of ádults comes this way.

The wise teacher will utilize every possible means of making the truth clearer, more vivid, more impressive, more interesting. And there is scarcely one out of the whole range of methods which cannot be successfully employed in teaching the Book of Job.

ORGANIZED CLASSES.—Of the first importance for holding, enlarging and obtaining the most benefit from a class, is a simple organization with president, secretary and treasurer and various committees. The invitation to become a member is extended by personal visit or by postal cards. Lists are made of those who are willing to take part in one way or another.

Some are willing to be called upon at any time without notice.

Some will make researches and report verbally or in writing.

Some are glad to come provided no questions are asked them.

All are welcome to ask questions at any time.

READINGS IN CHARACTER.—Job, because of its dramatic form and its discussions, is peculiarly adapted to this use in the class. The reading of the dialogues in the first two chapters by different persons, each representing one of the characters, and still more the reading by representative characters of selections from the discussions between Job and his friends giving the gist of the arguments, will give a fresh interest and new meaning to the discussion, beyond any previous expectation. It has been well said that no one has received the full power of the Scriptures till he has had the experience of their vocal interpretation. And whoever has had the privilege of hearing Professor Moulton, of Chicago, or Professor Duxbury, of Manchester, England, will realize the truth of this statement. In this book as much of the longer speeches has been given as can be used in the class hour, or the evening service. Should there be, however, a chance for a fuller reading it would be of great value.

BLACKBOARD DESIGNS.—Either on a blackboard, or window-shades, or strips of heavy wrapping paper, there should be made a simple scheme of the structure of the whole book, to be kept before the class during the course. And in addition the structure of the several divisions of the book should be given as each one is studied. These hold the attention, make clear the truth and fasten it in the memory.

DIFFERENT VERSIONS.—There is no small advantage in several members of the class having different versions before them, and noting the clearer meanings and better forms, and new views which thus come to light. The Revisions, English and American, give more new light on Job than on most of the other Old Testament books, in addition to their arrangement of the poetry in poetic form. Professor Moulton gives a fine arrangement. So does Cary in his poetic translation. Genung and several others give fresh poetic translations.

Professor Whitney writes in the *Bibliotheca Sacra* for July, 1902, p. 475, concerning the improvements made by the English and American Revisers, which are especially marked in the Book of Job: "The Book of Job seems to have been remarkably improved in this way. Its eloquence, always impressive, has seemed to acquire a new splendor with each touch of the corrector's hand. It is like the angel that has stood only half-emerged from the marble, but now has been chiselled out almost into full and magnificent release."[1]

UTILIZING THE CLASS MATERIAL.—Only a few persons in the majority of churches have sufficient time at their command to make the needed preparation for the best teaching on a new theme. Even in our church where there are between forty and fifty college graduates, it is difficult to find a teacher for the advanced lessons, through a long course. Every one is already overburdened. We find our way out in two directions: (1) We have a different teacher for each subject, notified long beforehand; (2) we utilize the material in the class for the research work of the different points in the lesson. Both of these methods add interest and power.

HOME WORK.—It will be impossible to obtain the best results from these studies unless the members of the class read the whole Book of Job carefully at home. While these lessons continue, it is an excellent plan to give one's devotional reading to the Book of Job. In our family, where at the time there were no very young children, we found great value in reading Job at family prayers during the weeks the lessons were in progress, each individual using a different version. Such occasional concentration on one book often produces a marvellous effect.

THE METHOD IN THIS VOLUME differs from any other course of the sort that has come under my notice. In addition to the formal plan, general statements, Bible references and questions, it offers suggestive thoughts, illustrations, practical applications, light from literature, and all that can give not only knowledge but inspiration and character-forming power, and help to higher daily living, very much as in my "Select Notes on the International Lessons."

[1] See Professor Whitney's illuminating articles on the Latest Translations of the Bible, in the *Bibliotheca Sacra* for April, July and October, 1902; January and April, 1903; April, 1904; and January and April, 1905.

And as this volume is for the teachers as well as for the members of the class, references are given to commentaries, literature, and various sources of information which the teacher can explore to his heart's content beyond the opportunities of his scholars. All these are not substitutes for work, but the means of more work and suggestions for further thought and illustration. They are no more "predigested food" or "means of cramming" than every book, conversation or sermon one reads or hears.

It is in just this line of character-forming truths made vivid and clear that most teachers stand in the greatest need of help, and where they are most likely to fail. Prof. Henry Van Dyke, in his "School of Life," writes from his own experience: "If a good book be, as Milton said, 'the precious life-blood of a master-spirit, embalmed and treasured,' still the sacred relic, as in the vial of St. Januarius at Naples, remains solid and immovable. It needs a kind of miracle to make it liquify and flow—the miracle of interpretation and inspiration—wrought most often by the living voice of a wise master, and communicating to the young heart the wonderful secret that some books are alive. Never shall I forget the miracle wrought for me by the reading of Milton's 'Comus' by my father in his book-lined study on Brooklyn Heights, and of Cicero's 'Letters' by Professor Packard in the Latin class at old Princeton."

My own experience tells the same story of "the miracle of interpretation and inspiration." And I trust that this little volume may be the means of that same wonder-work in the experience of others.

COMMENTS.—It would be impossible to include a full commentary in this volume; but three things will be included in our plan:

1. We give references to the best and most helpful commentaries.

2. We propose to call attention to the most striking and beautiful passages, not to

"Hold a farthing candle to the sun,"

but to summon busy people to view the sun itself.

We would not "each dark passage shun," provided there is an inner light in the dark passage which will shine out like a geode, when the seemingly dull and commonplace stone broken open by the hammer of a word of comment reveals a cluster of jewels.

We would call attention to those words and phrases which often have whole "poems, epics, idyls" hidden in them as the bud enfolds the rose; those oriental allusions, those metaphors which may be illumined as a light within a cathedral illumines the windows which, dull and vague to an observer without, become to one within pictures exquisitely beautiful in color and form.

3. We propose to give references to general literature which bears upon the subjects discussed, so far as the limits of our space and of our knowledge will allow.

These will be open doors to almost limitless study.

BIBLIOGRAPHY

1. For the Members of the Ordinary Class, as distinguished from critical scholars, I would place first, as most helpful, and as desirable to be in the possession of one or more of the members:

Professor Genung's "Epic of the Inner Life." Of all the books written upon Job, Genung's comes nearest to the real heart of the book. It contains a new poetical translation. ($1.25. Houghton & Mifflin.)

Professor Moulton's "Modern Reader's Bible; the Book of Job." The Revised Version arranged with his usual skill in dramatic form, with a peculiarly helpful introduction and brief illuminating notes. It is, however, very difficult to keep the connection of places with the ordinary chapters and verses. (50c. Macmillan.)

Dr. Samuel Cox (editor of *The Expositor*) has written the best and most fruitful "Commentary on the Book of Job," with a new translation. "An exposition which any man of ordinary culture may read with interest and pleasure." (15 shillings. Kegan Paul & Co., London.)

Dr. Otis Cary's "The Man Who Feared God for Naught." A metrical translation, in character arrangement, with "stage directions" which set forth the dramatic element; and with an interesting and helpful introduction. (Printed at the Orphan Asylum, Okayama, Japan. 50c. Revell.)

Prof. S. A. Martin's "The Man of Uz." Lessons for young Christians from the life of an ancient saint. For Young People's Societies. (50c. Presbyterian Board of Publication.)

William Blake's "Illustrations of the Book of Job." 21 plates. (1826.) Facsimile copies issued by Putnam (1902) at $4.00 (reduced to $2.00, net). An old-fashioned but interesting set of pictures.

2. Commentaries on Job, giving more or less of the critical processes and results.

By Watson, in "Expositor's Bible."

By Professor Davidson, in the "Cambridge Bible."

By Daniel Curry. (Methodist Book Concern, 1887.)

By Dr. Thomas Conant, including the translation by the Baptist Union. (1867.)

By Prof. Franz Delitzsch. (T. & T. Clark, Edinburgh.)

By Dr. Edgar C. S. Gibson, in "Westminster Commentaries." (2d edition, 1905, Methuen, London.)

"The Book of Job. Handbooks of Bible Series." Rev. James Aitken, M.A. (T. & T. Clark.)

Dillmann, "On the Text of Job."

Budde's late work on Job has an excellent review by Professor Cheyne in *The Expositor* for June, 1897.

Professor Driver's "Introduction to the Literature of the Old Testament."

Dr. Washington Gladden's "Seven Puzzling Bible Books." ($1.25. Houghton & Mifflin.)

The "International Critical Commentary on Job," by Prof. S. R. Driver, D.D., is in course of preparation. ($3.00. Scribners.)

3. MONOGRAPHS ON JOB:

Prof. Arthur Peake's "The Problem of Suffering in the Old Testament."

Walls' "The Oldest Drama in the World." (Methodist Book Concern.)

Rossiter Raymond's "Book of Job," with a metrical paraphrase, the outcome of his teaching the book to a Bible Class in Plymouth Church, Brooklyn. (Appleton.)

Dean Bradley's "Lectures on Job," delivered in Westminster Abby in 1885, 1886. (2d edition, Oxford University Press.)

Professor Royce's "Studies in Good and Evil; the Problem of Job." ($1.50. Appleton, 1899.)

Prof. George H. Gilbert's "The Poetry of Job," a rhythmical translation, with notes on the poetry of the book.

The Introduction to the "Book of Job," in the Temple Bible Series, misses the very heart of the poem. (50c. Lippincott.)

Principal Marshall's "The Book of Job," one volume of the "American Commentary." A full introduction and notes. (75c. American Baptist Publication Society, 1904.)

Prof. W. H. Green, "Arguments of the Book of Job Unfolded." (New York, 1874.)

Articles in Hastings' "Bible Dictionary," and in the "Encyclopædia Biblica."

Froude's Essay on Job, in 'Short Studies on Great Subjects." Vol. i.

4. SIDELIGHTS ON JOB:

Professor Butcher's "Harvard Lectures on Greek Subjects, Greece and Israel." ($2.25. Macmillan.)

J. B. Mozley's "Essays." Vol. ii.

Bushnell's "Moral Uses of Dark Things."

James Hinton's "The Mystery of Pain."

Charles Cuthbert Hall's "Does God Send Trouble?" ($1.00. Houghton & Mifflin.)

5. COMPARISONS AND CONTRASTS WITH OTHER LITERATURE:

Æschylus: Drama of "Prometheus Bound."

Sophocles: Drama of "Antigone."
Goethe: "Faust." Mephistopheles.
Dante: "Inferno" and "Purgatorio."
Milton: "Paradise Lost." Satan.
Shakespeare: "Hamlet;" "the Job of Shakespeare."
Browning: "The Ring and the Book."
Mrs. Browning: "Drama of Exile."
Spenser: "Fairy Queen."
Plato: "Republic," on Justice.
Sylvester: "Job Triumphant."
Quarles: "Job Militant."

In the Temple Bible, "Job and Ruth," can be found 208 references to Job by well-known writers in English literature.

"There exists in the church of St. Patrice, at Rouen, an interesting but little-known series of windows, whose subject is the Book of Job, as told in the first two and the last chapters."

In the Campo Santo at Genoa is a fine statue of Job and his friends.

INTRODUCTION

I. THE PROBLEM

THE problem, to throw light on which the Book of Job was written, is: **The Mystery of Suffering in God's World, in its Twofold Aspect—its Relation to God, and its Relation to Man.**

The first mystery lies in the difficulty, especially for one who is suffering, of believing that the God who rules this world of tragedies, of wars, of oppressions, of unspeakable cruelties, and intolerable agonies, is good and wise, a loving Father in Heaven. Is it strange that Omar Khayyam could see the world as described in his "Rubaiyat," making men

> "But helpless Pieces of the Game He plays
> Upon this chequer-board of Nights and Days.
>
> . . . .
>
> Who Man of baser earth did make
> And e'en in Paradise devise the snake." (Sts. lxix, lxxx.)

Can it be that a good and loving God rules this seemingly misgoverned world, where evil comes upon the evil and good alike; where the fire burns equally the martyr and the villain; and the storm overwhelms in the same ruin the pirate ship and the *Morning Star* freighted with missionaries and the Gospel; where the life of the best men seems to be a tragedy, and its crown a crown of thorns, while the wicked sometimes roll in wealth and sit on thrones?

Is God a mere Relentless Fate, imprisoned in His own laws? Is it a true picture which is described in Zola's "La Bête Humaine," of a railway train dragged by an engine whose driver has been killed, dashing at headlong speed into the midnight? "The train is the world, we are the freight, fate is the track, death is the darkness, God is the engineer—who is dead."

Is the representation of this world by Omar Khayyam according to fact?

Or can we find an explanation of this world of mingled good and evil in the Zoroastrian religion "dating more than twelve centuries before Christ, where in order to escape from making God responsible for evil, a dual principle was conceived, giving birth to the two brothers, Aurasmazda, the power for good, and Ahriman, the power of evil." (Raymond, "The Book of Job," p. 58.)

xviii

The soul cries out for a good God, not a mere "bright Essence Increate," not a mere "Power that makes for Righteousness," but a Loving Father. The soul needs faith in God, and love to God.

> "There was the Door to which I found no Key,
> There was the Veil through which I might not see."
> ("Rubaiyat" of Omar Khayyam, st. xxxii.)

Job's friends tried in a wrong way to find a solution. "For the theologian, next to the existence of a good God, the most fundamental question is the presence of pain and evil in a world he has ordered." (Prof. R. G. Moulton, Ph.D., "Modern Reader's Bible," p. v.)

The manward aspect of this problem is full of perplexity, conflict, and despair. The fact of such seemingly indiscriminate suffering throws a pall of darkness over the soul. It is the Sphinx's riddle,[1] which it is death not to solve. Who has not asked as the heathen did of the missionary, Why God not kill Devil?

When the quaint Sojourner Truth was seeking to free her children from slavery, and in direst extremity knew not where to turn for money or aid, she prayed: "O God, if I was as rich as you be, and you as poor as I be, I'd help you, you know I would. Now help me."

If God is so rich, why am I, his child, so poor?

If God is so strong, why does he permit my enemies—sin, temptation, disease, pain, death of my dearest, to overwhelm me, so that I must exclaim: All thy waves and thy billows have gone over me?

If God is so wise and good, why does he let disaster, disappointment, losses, heart-break, come upon us till it would seem as if the tempest would never be overpast, or the sun shine again?

THIS PROBLEM IS UNIVERSAL.—It confronts every individual at some time in his life. It belongs to every age. It belongs to the history of Israel as a people, to different periods of that history, to the Egyptian bondage, to the Exile, to the Maccabean period, and to the history of the Church. It is because of what Carlyle terms this "noble universality" that there is so great a variation among critics as to the age and date of the writing of the book.

---

[1] The Sphinx was a monster borrowed from Egyptian symbolism and was represented with the body of a winged lion and the breast and head of a human being. According to Hesiod the Sphinx took up her abode on a rock near Thebes in Egypt, and gave every passer-by the well-known riddle, "What walks on four legs in the morning, on two at noon, and on three in the evening?" She flung from the rock all who could not answer it. When Œdipus explained the riddle rightly, as referring to man in the successive stages of infancy, the prime of life, and old age, she flung herself down from the rock. See Harper's "Dictionary of Classical Literature and Antiquities." Brewer, "Dictionary of Phrase and Fable," gives a poetical version of the riddle:

> "What goes on four feet, on two feet, on three;
> But the more feet it goes on the weaker it be?"

THE BOOK OF JOB is the divine light shining on this problem giving all the lines of solution possible in the twilight of the early ages, to be seen at last in the full blaze following the dayspring Jesus brought from on high.

The Book of Revelation furnishes a most interesting parallel tc the Book of Job, and aids in its understanding. In both cases the beginning is happy and peaceful; then follows a long period of conflict; and in both the ending is a great and glorious success both in character and in the outward expression. (See Samuel Cox, D.D., "Commentary on the Book of Job," pp. 11–19; Prof. A. B. Davidson, D.D., in the "Cambridge Bible," pp. 23–29; Prof. John F. Genung, "The Epic of the Inner Life," pp. 11–15.)

II. THE LITERARY FORM

It is almost universally agreed that the basis of the Book of Job was an historical fact; that Job was a real man who underwent such severe trials and disasters that they made a lasting impression upon his age, and the ages following. Ezekiel (xiv, 14) and James (v, 11) both mention Job.[1]

The great majority of scholars stand upon Professor Davidson's statement that "the Poem reposes upon an historical tradition which the writer adopted as suitable for his moral purpose, and the outline of which he has preserved." ("Cambridge Bible," p. xiii.)

The opinion of most people half a century ago was that the book was a history, an exact reproduction of what was said and done. But aside from various other reasons no four or five persons casually brought together ever uttered extemporaneously such highly wrought poems, with such beautiful imagery—poems which (according to the "Cambridge Bible," p. xviii) "could only be the leisurely production of a writer of the highest genius" inspired by God.

Some years ago a gentleman who lived near the Wayside Inn in Sudbury told me, expressing a common belief, that Longfellow's "Tales of a Wayside Inn" were actually told by the Student, the Poet, the Theologian, the Musician, and the other characters assembled there; and that Mr. Longfellow returning to Cambridge wrote them out in poetic form. It occurred to me that possibly the Book of Job was written, at least in part, in that way. But in answer to inquiries as to the fact, Mr. Longfellow wrote me that "the tales were never told at Sudbury any more than the 'Canterbury Tales' were told on the way from London, or the 'Tales of a Traveller' at a Flemish inn. Howe's Tavern at Sudbury was chosen for its many associations, and for the beauty of its neighborhood. It was only a pleasant and convenient locality for the tales."

---

[1] Critics differ as to how far the story of Job has been idealized. See Prof. R. G. Moulton, "Modern Reader's Bible," p. vii; Rev. Otis Cary, "The Man Who Feared God for Naught," p. xi; Samuel Cox, D.D., "Commentary on Job," p. 11; Prof. A. B. Davidson, "Cambridge Bible," p. xiii. The arguments for regarding the book as a poem are given by Professor Davidson in "Cambridge Bible," p. xvii, etc. See also Daniel Curry, "The Book of Job," p. xxix.

So the sad experience of Job, his conflict and his final victory were the most perfect and fitting groundwork for teaching in the most effective way the great divine truths about the darkest problem that faces mankind.

As the parable of the Prodigal Son has had vastly more power than the same truths told in a didactic way, and is a perfect vehicle of divine inspiration; so when we realize that the Book of Job is a divinely inspired poem, drama or epic, founded on fact, and true to fact, to life, and to God, the whole book is lifted to a higher sphere, and given a more effective power.

It is well to consider how great are the gains to the right understanding of the Bible, from the fact, and the realization of the fact, that the Bible is written in such a variety of literary forms, so that every essential truth is presented to us in many ways—in prose statement, in story, in poetry, in dramatic presentation, in symbol, in metaphor, and especially in history and biography as actually lived out by men and nations. And this is necessary in order to guard against mistaken interpretations, errors, and half-truths, which are sure to arise from any single presentation. Moreover, we often have to consider the form of the literature in which any statement appears before we can, in many cases, determine the meaning and application. That Massachusetts governor who quoted Satan's words in Job as divine truth would never have done so if he had realized that the Book of Job was a dramatic poem. The pessimism in portions of Ecclesiastes, which Omar Khayyam has exaggerated, would never have been regarded as divinely authorized if its literary structure had been understood. (See Peloubet's "The Front Line of the Sunday-School," p. 223.)

In literary form the Book of Job is a combination of Prose and Poetry, such as Shakespeare frequently uses in his plays. The first two chapters, except one stanza, and the last chapter, from verse 7 to the end, are in prose.

The forms of poetic expression are very varied. It is dramatic, and yet is not strictly a drama, but "the lack of a theatre to specialize drama has caused the dramatic impulse to spread through other literary forms until epic, lyric, discourse, are all drawn together on a common basis of dramatic expression." "The whole range of literary expression" and "all the modes of thinking of which these forms (poetry and prose) are the natural vehicles" are combined in the Book of Job.[1] Hence Professor Moulton calls the book

A Dramatic Poem Framed in an Epic Story

Even "the philosophical discussion is also a dramatic debate." (See Prof. R. G. Moulton, D.D., "Modern Reader's Bible," pp. vi, vii.)

Prof. W. T. Davison says (in Hastings' "Bible Dictionary," art. "Job"): "The book is not a drama, nor a didactic poem, nor any composition of conventional form or shape, but . . . a law unto itself, which has influenced sub-

---

[1] For a full discussion of the metrical system of Job, see pp. 132–41 of Moulton, "Modern Reader's Bible."

sequent writers whose names stand among the highest in literature, yet who, by general consent, are merely from the literary point of view outsoared and outshone by their great prototype." (See A. B. Davidson, "Cambridge Bible," pp. 21, 22, and his earlier "Commentary on Job.")

It is to be noted that the structure of the book is itself exquisitely poetic and artistic, like the majestic conception of an entire cathedral as distinguished from the wealth and beauty of its details. The rapid change of scene from earth to heaven; the beautiful idyllic picture of Oriental prosperous life; the intermingling of divine and satanic and human agencies; the scenes and thoughts "fringed around with another world"; the dramatic dialogues; the unexpected entrance of the youthful Elihu; the coming of the storm during his speech; and the expression of its varying degrees of intensity, till it culminates in the whirlwind and the glory of the Shekinah, the voice of God from the whirlwind; the final steps toward the restoration of Job, and his ultimate success—all combine in a marvellous poetical structure, but perfectly natural, and all necessary to the solution of the problem.

The first prose chapters are as poetic in structure as the poetic portions.

The poem is full of poetic imagery, with lyrics of exquisite form and surprising beauty. "Only a close study of the book can give an idea of the richness and multitude of its metaphors, . . . its depth of human feeling." (Prof. W. T. Davison, in Hastings' "Bible Dictionary," art. "Job.")

The effect is increased by the variations in the length of the line.

Hebrew poetry is distinguished in two ways, by its parallelism of thought, and by its rhythm, time-beats, or tones. (See Prof. George H. Gilbert, "Poetry of Job," p. x; and Prof. G. A. Briggs, D.D., "Biblical Study," Chap. IX.)

"The Hebrew lines in Job generally have three tones, the only exceptions being fifty-nine two-toned, and eighty-five four-toned lines.

"The number of syllables belonging to the sphere of a single tone varies constantly, producing what would be designated, according to our canons of meter, a mingling of iambic, trochaic, dactylic and anapestic feet; but the rhythm is not often disturbed by this freedom."[1] The English translation is not always as melodious as the Hebrew.

---

[1] This difference in the number of syllables to each beat or tone is frequently seen in modern poetry as well as ancient. Take the hymn "Holy, Holy, Holy," and the music for it has to be written to accommodate the irregularity of the number of syllables to a beat. So in the first line of Cranch's quatrain there are four syllables to the first beat, two each to the second and third, and only one to the fourth.

> "Ma'nў̆ ăre thĕ/thoughts' thăt/come' tŏ/mē/
> In' my/lone'ly/mu'sing/,
> And' they/drift' so/strange' and/swift/
> There's' no/time' for/choo sing."/

Yet the beats are equal in time, and the lines are perfectly musical. The best prose always has a similar rhythm.

The most enlightening article I have ever seen on this subject is Poe's "Rationale of Verse."

Parallelism or thought-rhythm is the most distinctive characteristic of Hebrew poetry, and is found everywhere. For instance:

"There the wicked cease from troubling,
    And there the weary be at rest." (Job iii, 17.)

"Wilt thou harass a driven leaf?
    Wilt thou pursue the dry stubble?" (Job xiii, 25.)

(See Prof. R. G. Moulton on "The Psalms," and his "Literary Study of the Bible.")

III. THE EPIC OF THE INNER LIFE

While other writers on Job have suggested that "the action (of the poem) is internal and mental, and the successive scenes are representations of the varying moods of a great soul struggling with the mysteries of its fate " ("Cambridge Bible," p. xxi), it has remained for Prof. John F. Genung to set forth most perfectly and completely the real literary nature of the book, in such a way as to throw to one side many of the criticisms of its poetic form.

He calls the book "The Epic of the Inner Life."

"This poem centres in a hero, whose spiritual achievements it makes known to us. . . . It is a record of a sublime epic action, whose scene is not the tumultuous battle-field, nor the arena of rash adventure, but the solitary soul of a righteous man. . . . Under these discourses we are to trace not the building of a system, but the progress of a character, tried, developed, victorious. . . . Now in the Book of Job we have indeed a story, an action, but of very peculiar kind: the scene, so far as appears to the eye, only an ash-heap outside an Arab city, but to the inner view the soul of man, with all its warring passions, beliefs, convictions. It is the spiritual history of the man of Uz, his struggles and adventures, unknown to sense, but real to faith, as his fervid thoughts ' go sounding on, a dim and perilous way.' . . . Is it less truly epic than that conflict of temptation in the wilderness which Milton has sung—a conflict whose weapons were piercing words and whose battle-ground was the soul of the Son of Man?" (Pp. 18, 20, 21, 23, 25.)

It is in reality a kind of dramatically told epic poem describing a real human soul in its inner conflicts on the battle-field of the heart, its moral heroic achievements, and the final peace of victory. It is the history of a greater warfare than Homer's ten years' war around Troy. The greatest battles ever fought were on the battle-field within the soul of man. Compare Bunyan's "Capture of Mansoul."

Dean Bradley says: "Like Epic Poems it has a hero, a struggle, and a conquest. The hero like a Ulysses or an Æneas, gives his name to the Hebrew poem. . . . It represents in the sublimest and most striking of forms, a struggle and a triumph in which men of every age and every nation may claim an enduring interest." ("Lectures on Job," pp. 13, 14. Compare the construction of Tennyson's "In Memoriam.")

The study of the Book of Job as a mere "argument cunningly put together by a skilled reasoner" leaves it "beset with difficulties well-nigh insurmountable." (Genung, "Epic of the Inner Life," p. 4.) The critics see flaws and contradictions in the argument; they must add here and take away there, and see many a reviser's hand. But these difficulties are avoided when the book is studied as the fervent outpourings of a deeply troubled soul; for naturally in that case the progress of thought cannot be uniform, the colloquies cannot be reduced to syllogisms. They are the outpourings of deep feeling; they have the inconsistencies of a sufferer wrestling with a problem that he cannot solve; they are the outpourings of speakers whose feelings are sometimes at white heat. (See Hastings' "Bible Dictionary," p. 661.) "There is no life of man faithfully recorded but is a heroic poem of its sort, rhymed or unrhymed." (Carlyle, "Memoirs of the Life of Scott.")

Goethe says, "I never had an affliction which did not turn into a poem." Mrs. Browning's sonnet, "Perplexed Music," where a pale musician, on "a dulcimer of patience," could make only sad, perplexed, minor music with no measured tune, but the angels "smiled down from the stars and whispered, Sweet."

IV. UNITY AND METHOD OF COMPOSITION

There are two views as to the unity of the book according as the student looks upon it—

> from a Literary standpoint and atmosphere; or
> from a Critical standpoint and atmosphere.

1. From the literary and ethical standpoint the book is one complete and beautiful whole, by one inspired author of consummate genius. According to the *London Spectator* (speaking of Homer): "It is as impossible that a first-rate poem or work of art should be produced without a great master-mind to conceive the whole, as that a fine living bull should be developed out of beef sausages."

"As a whole, the Book of Job is intelligible, and, indeed, easily intelligible; as a piece of patchwork it defies explanation."

So Genung: "If the discourses of Elihu form no part of the original poem, but were added, as the critics assert nowadays, by a subsequent editor, then all I have to say is, I prefer to study the poem in its latest edition. From the point of view here taken, the writer who added such a finishing touch as this was a master in his art, one who could be fully trusted to compose the whole poem, as indeed I am willing to believe he did. In other words, I do not think the critics who would expel Elihu have made out their case. From their conception of the poem's scope and purpose he is in the way; they cannot help desiring his absence." ("Epic of the Inner Life," pp. 78, 79.)

But Elihu is as essential a part of the purpose and mission of the book as a hand or arm of a complete man. To leave him out takes away the emphasis on his solution of the problem, and that most poetical part of the book describing the coming of the storm out of which God speaks. There is no great poem extant of which it can be shown that it was composed by several authors at different periods.

Compare the case of Homer. About a century ago the long accepted tradition that the "Iliad" and "Odyssey" were by a single author named Homer, was broken. The "Iliad" was broken by Lackman into sixteen different lays, others taught that the "Iliad" had a Homeric kernel enlarged by additions by various authors. The two poems were compared by Paley to pictures of stained glass, made up by an artistic combination of handsome bits of older windows which fortune and time had shivered. But scholars, says President Strong, "are of late more and more arraying themselves on the side of the traditional view that both poems are substantially by the same author, and that this author is Homer. . . . Consider for a moment what demands the opposite hypothesis makes upon our credulity. Instead of one Homer, or two Homers, we are to believe in many Homers, each equal to the production of a poem which may ultimately constitute a part of the 'Iliad' or the 'Odyssey.' Are great poets then so plenty in human history?" (See Pres. A. H. Strong, D.D., "The Great Poets and their Theology," pp. 6–17; and Gladstone's "Homer.")

2. The larger number of critical scholars look upon Job as a composite work, some, like Davidson, confining the later addition to the speech of Elihu; others, like Cheyne, making out many additions in all parts of the book, "so that the book may have been centuries in coming to its present form," like many a large house built by different persons at different periods, in different styles of architecture; or possibly like the Cathedral of Cologne which was complete after seven centuries from the original plans.

It is easy to see that they have strong arguments from certain points of view—the third round of speeches is incomplete; Elihu comes in without announcement, and is not referred to at the conclusion; chapters xxvi–xxviii seem to contain contradictions as at present arranged; the closing chapter has peculiarities of its own.

The arguments for this view in some of its phases are given in almost every book on Job, and can be studied by those who are interested in these questions. Davidson thinks that for wholesale reorganization there is no external evidence. Moulton obviates some of the difficulties by rearranging chapters xxvi–xxviii. Genung obviates others by his view of the book as an epic of the inner life, "for we are not concerned to keep the different stages of a spiritual conflict in strict logical unity." They never are in such unity.

3. It is well to keep in mind that the various views of the composition and growth do not necessarily limit the value of the book, or interfere with the fact of its inspiration, though they may modify the theory and method of inspiration.

4. For Bible class purposes, ethical and spiritual, the book must be treated as a whole, as it stands, and all the variant theories of its composition be left in the background.

5. It is not improbable that the author used the story of Job as Shakespeare uses old tales as the basis of some of his plays. These facts are common property, but no one dreams of discussing the sources of Shakespeare's inspiration to the neglect of Shakespeare himself. It has ever been the prerogative of genius to take the baser metals and transmute them into gold.

Browning's "Ring and the Book," according to his own statement to an Englishman, was founded on an old manuscript story he found in Rome.

"When Mrs. Humphry Ward published 'Lady Rose's Daughter' some critic discovered that the central character was a portrait of a real French historical personage (Mlle. de l'Espinasse), introduced by the author for the purpose of showing the development of a certain character under certain peculiar circumstances." But Mrs. Ward did not tell us so. The same is said to be true of her "Marriage of William Ashe."

It is probable that Homer's "Iliad" was a growth which Homer's genius brought into perfect flower. It doubtless grew under his own hand, as Goethe in one of his letters to Schiller cites different versions of his own poems.

Moreover, such a book as Job must have been written in a time of general thought and interest and discussion of the problem. The great masterpieces of literature are like the highest mountain peaks, which emerge not from a sandy plain, but from a mountainous country.

In the words of Genung:

"Genius may indeed be a mighty tree, growing from an unseen germ to be the one commanding object of the plain; but it is rooted in the same soil that nourishes the shrubs at its feet. A great work of literature both feeds its age and is fed by it. What the book returns, in transmuted and vitalized form, to its generation is what it has already gathered out of the hopes and needs and problems that surround it. Not that the highest literature is merely the echo of the people's surging thought, and no more; we cannot say this of Tennyson and Browning and Whittier and Emerson to-day: it is rather the utterance of those who, making the universal cause their own, stand nearest the light, and bring the people's inarticulate longings to expression. . . . In them we hear, not one man alone, but the vast body of the time, pervaded by a spirit of hope or doubt or inquiry; a spirit voiceless, until the Æolian strings of the poet's heart feel and answer to its breathings." ("Epic of the Inner Life," pp. 89, 90.)

V. AUTHOR

The authorship of the Book of Job is entirely unknown. No hint any-where is given as to who wrote the book. He is the "Great Unnamed," inspired by the Holy Spirit of God. "It is a point on which even this omniscient age must be content to remain in doubt."

VI. THE AGE AND DATE OF THE BOOK

1. The period when Job lived, to which his personal story belongs, the scene of the drama, is almost universally understood to be the age of the Patriarchs some two thousand years before Christ. But this gives no information as to the time when the book was written, any more than the date of "King Lear" or of "Julius Cæsar" tells us when Shakespeare wrote his plays.

2. As to the period when the Book of Job was written scholars widely differ. Nearly all, at present, think that the Jewish belief that the book was written by Moses during his forty years in the desert is unfounded, although Moses needed its consolations as much as any one has needed them since.

The majority of authorities place the writing of the book somewhere between the age of Solomon and the Exile, some at one period and some at another as to them appear the circumstances which call for such light on their troubles. Genung ("Epic of the Inner Life," pp. 90, 118), Cary ("The Man Who Feared God for Naught," pp. xii–xx) and Ewald place it in the age of Uzziah and Hezekiah. Cox ("Commentary on the Book of Job," pp. 6–9), Curry ("The Book of Job," pp. xiv–xxi), Bradley ("Lectures on Job," pp. 169–77) and Davidson ("Cambridge Bible," pp. lv–lxviii—as the earliest possible date) place it about the age of Solomon. Cheyne ("Job and Solomon"—for the last revision), Wellhausen and Davidson (by preference) about the time of the captivity.

For a discussion of the reasons for their choice, study the above authors.

"The strongest argument (for a late date), and perhaps the only one which is really conclusive, is drawn from the subject matter." The theme here dis-cussed and the manner of its discussion "necessitate a long previous history." The problems are old, but they could not be raised in the manner disp·ayed by Job without a previous religious history of considerable duration. And "the history of the Old Testament shows that only at a comparatively late period were these maxims (of the current explanations of the facts of life given by Job's three friends) questioned." (W. T. Davison in Hastings' "Bible Dic-tionary," art. "Job.")

On the other hand, sufficient account is not taken by most scholars of the fact that the whole atmosphere of the poem as it now stands is patriarchal and ancient. It is far more like the atmosphere of Genesis and Judges than like

Kings and the Prophets. As Froude remarks: "The material is so rich and pregnant that we might with little difficulty construct out of it a complete picture of the world as then it was: its life, knowledge, arts, habits, superstitions, hopes and fears." (Froude, "Short Studies on Great Subjects," p. 211.) And there is not a single reference or allusion to anything that might not have existed in those early days. The reference to the laws in Deuteronomy, even if it were true that Deuteronomy is a late book, are similar to those in the "Code of Hammurabi," dated by scholars even earlier than Abraham. The references to captivities and troubles were as true of an earlier as of a later period. As Renan remarks, it is "impossible to believe that any poet of Solomon's age should have thrown himself back into an age so distant and have maintained the tone throughout. Such a feat has never been achieved; such a feat was wholly foreign to the spirit of the time." (Samuel Cox, D.D., "Commentary on Job," p. 9.)

It is still more marvellous, bordering on the inconceivable, that an author living in the time of the prophets, of the temple, and of the Psalms, and in all the light which Israel's history could shed upon the problem, should utterly ignore all this divine light and confine himself to that which was known in the earlier ages, before a single book of Scripture was written.

Therefore the argument for an earlier time, probably at some period in the age of the Judges, is stronger than all the arguments for a later age.

Though Job is to be classed with the Wisdom Literature of the Bible, there is no regular, orderly progression of great books such as one might naturally expect. There is no regular progression of Homer, Dante, Shakespeare, Tennyson. And the theme of the Book of Job must have puzzled men even long before Abraham. It belongs to man as man.

Note that while the age or period of the writing of Job is an interesting and enlightening question, yet practically it has no especial bearing upon the subject of the book, and is of no further account in our studies.

VII. RELATION TO OTHER SCRIPTURES

An interesting study can be made by comparison of passages in Job with similar ones in other portions of Scripture, in addition to those especially relating to the themes we consider in the progress of our studies.

For instance, Job himself is referred to in Ezekiel xiv. 14; James v. 11. Job xxxi. 33 refers to Adam; xxii. 16 perhaps to the Flood; Job i. 21; ii. 10 remind us of the prayer of Habakkuk. Ps. xxxvii and xxxviii suggest a general comparison with Job.

Compare

Job iii. 3–10 with Jer. xx. 14–18.	Job xiii. 28 with Isa. l. 9.
Job vi. 15 with Jer. xv. 18.	Job xiv. 11 with Isa. xix. 5.
Job vii. 17, 18 with Ps. viii. 4.	Job xv. 35 with Isa. lix. 4.
Job ix. 18 with Lam. iii. 15.	Job xvi. 13 with Lam. iii. 12.
Job xii. 4 with Jer. xx. 7.	Job xxviii. 28 with Eccl. xii. 13.
Job xii. 9 with Isa. xli. 20.	Job xxx. 9 with Lam. iii. 14.

NEW TESTAMENT ON OLD TESTAMENT PROBLEMS.

Job i. 9–11, 22 compare 2 Cor. vi. 4–6.
Job iii. 17 compare Matt. xi. 28–30; Rev. xxi. 27.
Job v. 17 compare Heb. xii. 6–11.
Job vii. 21 compare Rom. viii. 1.
Job ix. 33 compare Heb. i. 1–3.
Job xiv. 14 }
Job xix. 25–27 } compare 1 Cor. xv. 42–57.
Job xxi. 15 compare Matt. vi. 33; 1 Tim. vi. 6; Heb. xi. 6.
Job xxiii. 3 compare John xiv. 9 10.
Job xxiii. 10 compare 1 Pet. i. 7.
Job xxv. 4 compare Rom. v. 1.
Job xxxiii. 29–30 compare James i. 2, 3, 12; Rom. v. 3, 4.
Job xxxv. 10 compare Acts xvi. 25, 26.

CHOICE PORTIONS
(to be learned by heart).

Job iii. 17.	Job xviii. 5.	Job xxviii. 12–15, 23, 28.
Job iv. 13–19.	Job xix. 25–27.	Job xxix. 15.
Job v. 17, 18.	Job xxiii. 10.	Job xxxiii. 14–30.
Job xi. 7–9.	Job xxv. 4–6.	Job xxxviii. 11.
Job xiv. 14.	Job xxvi. 14.	Job xlii. 5, 6.

VIII. STRUCTURE OF THE BOOK

We will understand the meaning of the book best by noticing its peculiar structure.

It consists of five divisions:

1. Chapters i and ii, the prologue, in prose, the story on which the rest of the book is founded. It consists of five scenes, some on earth and some in heaven. The speakers are Jehovah, Job, Satan, four Messengers Job's wife.

2. Chapters iii–xxxi, in poetic form, the colloquy between Job and his three friends, continued through three rounds. Besides these there was an audience of neighbors, citizens, children, visitors, rabble.

3. Chapters xxxii–xxxvii. The Oration of Elihu. Poetry. Job, his three friends and citizens for audience. The oration was cut short by the storm.

4. Chapters xxxviii–xli. God speaks from the whirlwind. Poetry. Job, his three friends, Elihu, and citizens for audience.

5. Chapter xlii. 1–6. Poetry. Brief colloquy between the Lord and Job. Verses 7–17, prose. The complete restoration of Job. His spiritual and material history.

Now corresponding to these five divisions are the five solutions of the problem. So long as we have looked for only one solution, in the usual way, the mystery was unexplained, for there is no one solution that can explain all. It takes all five.

The solution of Part I is that sometimes trouble is **A Test.**

The solution of Part II is that sometimes it is **A Punishment.**

The solution of Part III is that it is **A Discipline.**

The solution of Part IV is that it is sometimes **An Insoluble Mystery.**

The solution of Part V is that the good man always comes to **True Success** at last. His life is never a tragedy.

Note that these solutions are the only conceivable solutions. Jesus Christ brought life and immortality to light, but so far as this problem is concerned his message flows in these five channels. What in Job was seen in the twilight Jesus shows us flooded with the light of the morning sun. The mountains and valleys, the forests and the rivers are the same in both, but what was a shadowy outline in Job is revealed in blessed clearness, in heavenly color, and absolute certainty in Christ.

"The Book of Job is about as long as Shakespeare's 'Hamlet'; like that Drama, it has five acts which are arranged in twenty-one scenes." (Walls, "The Oldest Drama in the World," p. 17.)

PART	LITERARY FORM	CHAPTERS	CHARACTERS	METHOD	SOLUTION
I	Prose	I and II	Jehovah Sons of God The Adversary Job. Job's wife 4 Messengers	Historic basis Visions 5 scenes	A Test
II	Poetry	III-XXXI	Job Bildad Eliphaz Zophar Brothers —— Citizens Neighbors Rabble	Discussions 3 cycles	Punishment
III	Poetry	XXXII-XXXVII	Elihu same audience	Oration coming of the storm	Discipline
IV	Poetry	XXXVIII-XLII 1-6	God speaks through his works	Voice out of the whirlwind	Faith in God
V	Prose	XLII. 7-17	God Job. Three Friends Relatives	Divine approval	Final Success

In teaching, this DIAGRAM should be enlarged on blackboard or chart, and kept before the class during the whole session.

PERSONS AND SCENES

PERSONS

Jehovah

Sons of God

The Adversary

Job, a wealthy sheik

Job's wife

A field hand

A shepherd

A drover

A house servant

Eliphaz, a venerable sheik from Teman

Bildad, a scholar from Shuah

Zophar, a prince of Naamah

Elihu, a young chief from Buz

Job's brothers

Job's sisters

Neighbors

Citizens

Boys

Rabble

SCENES

Job's home at Uz, a walled town surrounded by
broad fields

The council in heaven

A huge ash heap outside the walls

A great storm

A sacrifice and prayer

Job's home at Uz

PART I

THE HISTORICAL BASIS OF THE POEM.
PROSE. (Chapters i and ii.)

A SERIES OF FIVE SCENES

Changing from earth to heaven and back again. One of the most dramatic portions of the book.

TIME : Several weeks or months.

SCENES: Job's home at Uz. The council in heaven.

CHARACTERS: Jehovah. Sons of God. The Adversary. Job. Messengers. Job's Wife.

FIRST SOLUTION OF THE PROBLEM: SOMETIMES AFFLICTIONS ARE SENT AS A TEST OF CHARACTER

RESEARCH QUESTIONS

(To be assigned the previous lesson to various members of the class. Topics for discussion in the class.)

1. The geography of the lesson.

2. The character of Job, as stated at the beginning and end of the book, and as learned from what he says, especially in chapter xxxi.

3. Why is Job represented as so perfect? its bearing on the solution of the problem.

4. Why were the scenes in heaven concealed from Job?

5. The character of Satan, as revealed here and in other parts of the Bible.

6. The character of Job's wife.

7. The two sources of Job's afflictions—from man and from nature. Do these sources make any difference in our feelings and perplexity concerning our troubles?

8. Why is trouble from sickness and pain a severer test of character than loss of property?

9. The aggravation of affliction from the misjudgments of relatives and friends.

10. How does suffering reveal us to ourselves?

11. How does the way we bear trouble test our character before the world?

12. Does God send trouble? Report on C. Cuthbert Hall's book of that name.

13. What is God's relation to trouble that comes to us through bad men? Bible references.

14. What is God's relation to trouble that comes to us through his laws of nature? Bible references.

15. What part has Satan in our afflictions?

16. Bible instances of trouble coming upon good men.

17. Hymns expressing the truths of this portion of the Book of Job.

SCENE I.—EARTH:

Job at home, prosperous, peaceful.

SCENE II.—HEAVEN:

Council of Sons of God. Jehovah. Satan.
Satan goes on his mission.

SCENE III.—EARTH:

JOB'S HOME
at Uz.

Herder from SABEANS.
Shepherd from LIGHTNING.
Drover from CHALDEANS.
House servant from CYCLONE

SCENE IV.—HEAVEN:

Council of Sons of God. ⎱ Jehovah. Satan.
Second meeting.   ⎰   Report of Satan.

SCENE V.—EARTH:

An ash heap. Job a leper. Friends, relatives, citizens.

THE LAND OF JOB

As for the scene of the story, history, tradition, and the indications of the poem all point to the Hauran as the country in which Uz was situated. This is accepted by all scholars.

The Sea of Galilee and the upper Jordan are west of the Hauran; the Syrian desert extending toward the Euphrates is its eastern boundary; the Syrian mountains are on the north; and on the south are Moab, Arabia, and Edom. It is within easy reach of Damascus on the north.

The Arabs who to-day live in the district claim it as "the land of Job."

It is the country where most of the Abrahamides (descendants of Abraham other than through Isaac) found their homes.

It is to-day rich in the kind of wealth of which Job was possessed. It is exposed to the same kind of raids, and presents the same natural features of gorges and ravines whose treacherous streams the poet describes. From the desert come the same kinds of deluges of sudden rain and whirlwinds.[1]

The *Chaldeans* belonged to the region of the Euphrates. They were originally a robber tribe, and roamed for plunder as far west as Palestine. The *Sabeans* were a tribe of the desert Arabs, and accustomed to raid the cultivated lands.

SCENE I. JOB AT HOME

Job lived in the walled[2] town of Uz, with broad pastures and cultivated lands extending in every direction. He was very wealthy, with great herds and flocks, and a vast retinue of officers and servants. He was a prince, "the greatest of all the children of the East." His sons and daughters were settled not far away, and partook of his prosperity. He was a man in the very prime of life. His 3,000 camels imply that he was a "princely merchant, sending out large caravans to trade in the cities of the East." Thus is presented before us a beautiful picture of "the simple life," of well-earned prosperity, of serene peace, of deep piety, and wide usefulness. An ideal life of those days.

What is the truth in the following statement as regards this earlier portion of Job's life? "All this is life's crown," we say. "No," says the great artist, "it is not yet life's beginning."

THE CHARACTER OF JOB.—We learn this from two sources:

1. The testimony of Jehovah. Job was "a perfect and an upright man, one that feareth God and escheweth (Am. Rev. 'turneth away from') evil." (Job i. 8; ii. 3.) Evil was repulsive to him. "There is none like him in the earth." "He holdeth fast his integrity" in spite of his sufferings. "In all

---

[1] For further information see Cox, "Commentary on the Book of Job," p. 10; Curry, "The Book of Job," p. xxvi and Appendix; Raymond, "The Book of Job," pp. 25-36.

[2] It was the Oriental custom, as in many primitive peoples, for farmers to live in walled cities for safety, and to go out thence to their daily labors in vineyards and pastures.

this did not Job sin with his lips." (Job ii. 10.) Compare James (iii. 2):
"If any stumbleth not in word, the same is a perfect man." (Why?)

Note that Job did not gain this goodness and character without victory
over temptation. It was not mere innocence, it was character wrought out in
the presence of trial. Wealth and power often furnish the severest temptations
to pride, worldliness, selfishness, abuse of power, fleshly lusts.

> "Satan now is wiser than of yore
> And tempts by making rich, not making poor."
> > (Pope, "Moral Essays," iii. 351.)

2. We learn the character of Job from the testimony he gives under oath
in chapter xxxi, which Moulton calls his "Oath of Clearing." He was pure in
heart; he was honest to the core; he refused to oppress the poor; he was generous;
he aided the fatherless and made the widow's heart sing for joy; he did not
trust in his riches; he was an upright judge; he loved his enemies; he was hospitable to strangers; he made no dishonest gains; he was faithful and true to his
God.

Job was a gentleman of the old school. He was the Sir Galahad among
the Knights of the Round Table. He was not a recluse or an ascetic, for he
did not disapprove of his children's feasts, but simply guarded against their
dangers.

> "His life was gentle; and the elements
> So mixed in him, that Nature might stand up
> And say to all the world, This was a Man."
> > (Shakespeare, "Julius Cæsar," v. 5.)

> "A combination and a form indeed
> Where every god did seem to set his seal
> To give the world assurance of a man."
> > (Shakespeare, "Hamlet," iii. 4.)

> "A creature such
> As to seek through the regions of the earth
> For one his like, there would be something failing
> In him that should compare. I do not think
> That such an outward and such stuff within
> Endows a man but he."
> > (Quoted in Cox, "Commentary on Job," p. 14.)

> "The blessings of her quiet life
> Fell on us like the dew;
> And good thoughts where her footsteps pressed
> Like fairy blossoms grew."
> > (Whittier, "Gone.")

For a discussion of Job's patience, see under Part II.

THE VALUE of such an ideal character held up before the people for ages was very great. It was a perpetual educational force. It was a living example of the Ten Commandments, reinforcing every one. Dr. Parkhurst remarks, "While books can teach, personality only can educate." "The most influential thing in the world," says Professor Whitney, "is, we suppose, what men see in other people's lives." "No nobler feeling," says Carlyle, "than admiration for one higher than himself dwells in the breast of man. It is to this hour, and at all hours, the vivifying influence in man's life." ("Heroes and Hero Worship," The Hero as Divinity, p. 10.)

"There could not be a national history (according to Edersheim, "Life of Christ," vol. ii, Chap. IX), nor even romance, to compare with that by which a Jewish mother might hold her child entranced."

> "As the Grecian mother to the child upon her knee
> Sang of the land's heroic songs,
> Sang of Thermopylæ, of Marathon,
> Of proud Platæa's day
> Until the neighboring hills, from peak to peak,
> Answered the resounding lay."

SCENE II. IN THE UNSEEN WORLD. THE SONS OF GOD AS-
SEMBLED IN COUNCIL. (Job i. 6-12.)

Enter SATAN, *the* ADVERSARY.[1]

(This scene is a poetic expression of the real facts which belong to every age. Satan sums up the feeling of bad men the world over.)

READINGS IN CHARACTER.

JEHOVAH (*to* SATAN).

"Whence comest thou?"

THE ADVERSARY.

"From going to and fro in the earth, and from walking up and down in it."

JEHOVAH.

"Hast thou considered my servant Job? for there is none like him in the earth, a perfect and an upright man, one that feareth God, and escheweth evil."

---

[1] The best man, the most unlike Satan, should be chosen to read the part of Satan, just as in the Oberammergau Passion Play the part of Judas was taken by a man who, when some visitor asked him to do a dishonorable act, replied, "I am Judas only in the play."

THE ADVERSARY.

> "Doth Job fear God for naught? Hast thou not made an hedge about him and about his house, and about all that he hath, on every side? thou hast blessed the work of his hands, and his substance is increased in the land. But put forth thine hand now, and touch all that he hath, and he will renounce thee to thy face."

JEHOVAH.

> "Behold all that he hath is in thy power; only upon himself put not forth thine hand."

So Satan went forth from the presence of the Lord.

Take note that Job is entirely unconscious of this scene, and of the reasons why affliction is sent upon him. And this was necessary in order to make the test. If there had been no mystery, no unexplained evil, the whole character of the test would have been different. It is one thing to suffer evil as a martyr or a hero; it is a very different thing to trust and love God amid the inexplicable mysteries of sorrow and loss.

The reasons for Job's sufferings are revealed to the reader in order that he may comprehend the whole action of the poem, that he alone may see the working out of the problem, from the divine point of view. He sees from the first what Job and his friends could not so easily understand, that there are other reasons for sorrow than the punishment for sin, and other sources of calamity than the wickedness of the sufferer.

SONS OF GOD.—Those spirits who inherit his nature, work his will, are in entire sympathy with his character and plans.

> "Who at his bidding speed
> And post o'er land and ocean without rest."
> (Milton, "Sonnet on his Blindness.")

Take note how God delights in the good man, rejoices as his "angels rejoice over one sinner that repenteth." (See Luke xv. 7, 10.)

SATAN, THE ADVERSARY.—The adversary of good both in God and man.

From the story as given here we learn (1) that he went to and fro in the earth, not to find good, but evil, and that is one Cain-mark of a bad being. A distinguished American preacher once said, "I thank God that I love the good ten thousand times more than I hate the evil." That is an angel-mark of goodness.

(2) The adversary did not believe in the existence of good, for he found none in his own heart and experience. Another sign of an evil character.

(3) The adversary loved to do evil, to tempt, to injure men, to bring ruin, to destroy men's faith in goodness.

Now these are the characteristics of Satan found all through the Scriptures, revealed more and more fully, expressed in different ways under different circumstances, but the same "old serpent, the Devil," who tempted Adam and who tempted Christ.

A brief study of the Scriptural representations will reveal to us the nature of our adversary.

Old Testament: Gen. iii. 1; 1 Chron. xxi. 1; Zech. iii. 1.

New Testament: Matt. iv. 1–11; xiii. 19, 39; Luke iv. 6; xiii. 16; xxii. 31; John viii. 38–44; xii. 31; xiii. 2; Eph. vi. 11, 12; 2 Tim. ii. 26, etc.

Moulton ("Modern Reader's Bible," p. 147) makes Satan a general Inspector, or Guardian of the earth, suspicious, but without malignity, "an adversary only in the sense in which any inspector or examiner is opposed to those on whom he exercises his office."

Is this the representation in Job? (See Samuel Cox, "Commentary on Job," pp. 14, 15; Prof. John F. Genung, "Epic of the Inner Life," pp. 32, 134; "Cambr dge Bible," p. 7.)

"But of this be sure—
To do aught good will never be our task,
But ever to do ill our sole delight.
. . . .
And out of good still to find means of evil."
(Milton, "Paradise Lost," 1. 158–65.)

Satan came among the sons of God, not as Apollyon, but as an angel of light.[1] "The prince of darkness is a gentleman." ("King Lear.") Otherwise he would be a fool as well as a villain, and be far less dangerous.

"His form had not yet lost
All his original brightness, nor appeared
Less than archangel ruined."
(Milton, "Paradise Lost," 1. 591–93.)

SCENE III. A SUDDEN CHANGE TO JOB'S HOUSE. (Job i. 13–22.)

JOB *sitting quietly in the magnificence of a great Oriental chief.* Dr. Walls ("The Oldest Drama in the World," p. 22) may be right in his picture: "*The messengers in this scene enter in great excitement, and drenched with rain through which they came. The fire from heaven which consumed the sheep and the wind from the wilderness which smote the four corners of the house, were perhaps the lightning and the cyclone of one storm.*"

---

[1] Compare Milton's description of Satan. Goethe, in "Faust," draws his portrait of Mephistopheles and founds his prologue "wholly on the ideas of this incident in Job." Compare the Satan in Bickersteth's "Yesterday, To-day and Forever"; Mrs. Browning's Satan in her "Drama of Exile"; Byron's Satan in his "Vision of Judgment"; Dante's Satan, "a horrible, symbolic monster." See Raymond, "Book of Job," pp. 60–62.

READINGS IN CHARACTER.

Enter FIRST MESSENGER, *in great haste.*

FIRST MESSENGER, *a herder from distant pastures (speaking excitedly to* JOB).

"The oxen were ploughing, and the asses feeding beside them;
and the Sabeans fell upon them, and took them away;
yea, they have slain the servants with the edge of the
sword; and I only am escaped   [*Enter* SECOND MESSENGER.]
alone to tell thee."

SECOND MESSENGER, *a shepherd from the fields.*

"The fire of God is fallen from heaven, and hath burned up
the sheep, and the servants, and consumed them; and I
only am escaped alone to tell   [*Enter* THIRD MESSENGER.]
thee."

THIRD MESSENGER, *from the edge of the desert.*

"The Chaldeans made three bands, and fell upon the camels,
and have taken them away, yea, and slain the servants
with the edge of the sword;
and I only am escaped alone   [*Enter* FOURTH MESSENGER.]
to tell thee."

FOURTH MESSENGER, *a house servant from town.*

"Thy sons and thy daughters were eating and drinking
wine in their eldest brother's house: and behold there
came a great wind from the wilderness, and smote the
four corners of the house, and it fell upon the young
men, and they are dead; and I only am escaped alone to
tell thee."

THE EFFECT ON JOB.—Job stood the test. He rent his mantle and shaved
his head, "conventional and altogether appropriate forms of expressing his deep
sense of his losses," while his falling down, the Oriental attitude of worship,
and his worship of God, showed his unshaken faith and allegiance to God. He
went to his one source of comfort. Clouds and darkness surrounded the
Providence of God; but he knew that there was a silver lining on the other side,
and that in spite of all God is good.

JOB (*crushed at first, and lying prone in the dust*).

"Naked came I out of my mother's womb,
And naked shall I return thither." [1]

(*Then after a pause he regains his faith, and rises up.*)

"The Lord gave and the Lord hath taken away;
Blessed be the name of the Lord."

In all this Job sinned not, nor charged God with foolishness.

Then

"*The morning stars sang together,
And all the sons of God shouted for joy.*"

(Job xxxviii. 7.)

SCENE IV. THE UNSEEN WORLD. (Job ii. 1-6.)

The SONS OF GOD *again assembled in council.*

THE ADVERSARY *returning from his experimental test of* JOB.

READINGS IN CHARACTER.

JEHOVAH (*to* THE ADVERSARY).

"From whence comest thou?"

THE ADVERSARY.

"From going to and fro in the earth, and from walking up
and down in it."

JEHOVAH.

"Hast thou considered my servant Job? for there is none
like him in the earth, a perfect and an upright man, one
that feareth God, and escheweth evil: and he still holdeth
fast his integrity, although thou movedst me against him,
to destroy him without cause."

THE ADVERSARY.

"Skin for skin, yea, all that a man hath will he give for his
life. But put forth thine hand now, and touch his bone
and his flesh, and he will renounce thee to thy flesh."

JEHOVAH.

"Behold, he is in thine hand; only spare his life."

---

[1] So Paul (1 Tim. vi. 7): We brought nothing into the world, for neither can we carry anything out.

"The general sense of 'skin for skin' is clear enough, but the exact force of the proverb is not easy to catch." The meaning becomes clearer by comparison with some ancient proverbs quoted by Cox. The Arabic proverb "a hide for a hide," i. e., nothing without a full equivalent. The Jewish proverb, "One gives one's skin to save one's skin," i. e., gives a part to save the rest, "but gives all to save his life." Satan recognizes no good motive, but thinks Job would make a bargain with God and by giving up his property save his life, which includes health and whatever makes life worth living.

SCENE V. (1) THE CITY OF UZ. JOB'S HOUSE. (Job ii. 7–10.)

SATAN comes from the council of the SONS OF GOD and brings upon JOB, in some natural way, the most distressing disease possible, including not only pain, but depression of soul, separation from all that he loves, disfigurement and disgrace in the eyes of all around him.

JOB'S DISEASE.—It is generally agreed that the disease of Job was the leprosy called Elephantiasis, so named because the swollen limbs and the black and corrugated skin of those afflicted by it resemble those of the elephant. It is said by ancient authors, as Pliny, to be peculiar to Egypt, but it is found in other hot countries such as the Hijâz, and even in northern climates as Norway. It is said to attack the limbs first, breaking out below the knees and gradually spreading over the whole body. We are probably to consider, however, that Job was smitten "from the sole of his foot unto his crown" all at once. Full details of its appearance and the sensations of those affected may be gathered from the Book, though, being poetically coloured, they will hardly bear to be read like a page from a handbook of Pathology. The ulcers were accompanied by an itching so intolerable that a piece of potsherd was taken to scrape the sores and remove the feculent discharge, ii. 8. The form and countenance were so disfigured by the disease that the sufferer's friends could not recognise him, ii. 12. The ulcers seized the whole body both without and inwardly, xix. 20, making the breath fetid, and emitting a loathsome smell that drove every one from the sufferer's presence, xix. 17, and made him seek refuge outside the village upon the heap of ashes, ii. 8. The sores, which bred worms, vii. 5, alternately closed, having the appearance of clods of earth, and opened and ran, so that the body was alternately swollen and emaciated, xvi. 8. The patient was haunted with horrible dreams, vii. 14, and unearthly terrors, iii. 25, and harassed by a sensation of choking, vii. 15, which made his nights restless and frightful, vii. 4, as his incessant pains made his days weary, vii. 1–4. His bones were filled with gnawing pains, as if a fire burned in them, xxx. 30, or as if his limbs were tortured in the stocks, xiii. 27, or wrenched off, xxx. 17. He was helpless, and his futile attempts to rise from the ground provoked the merriment of the children who played about the heap where he lay, xix. 18. The disease was held incurable, though the patient might linger many years, and his hopelessness of recovery made him long for death, iii. 20 and often. (Prof. A. B. Davidson, in "Cambridge Bible," in loco.)

(2) OUTSIDE THE CITY WALLS

JOB *departs from his house and goes outside the city walls, because persons with this loathsome and infectious disease were not allowed within. We next see* JOB *lying on the city ash-mound, called a* Mezbele. "*The dung which is heaped upon the Mezbele of the Hauran villages is not mixed with straw, which in that warm and dry land is not needed for litter, and it comes mostly from solid-hoofed animals, as the flocks and oxen are left over-night in the grazing places. It is carried in baskets in a dry state to this place before the village, and usually burnt once a month. . . . The ashes remain. . . . If the village has been inhabited for centuries the Mezbele reaches a height far overtopping it. The winter rains reduce it into a compact mass, and it becomes by and by a solid hill of earth. . . . The Mezbele serves the inhabitants for a watchtower, and in the sultry evenings for a place of concourse, because there is a current of air on the height. There all day long the children play about it; and there the outcast, who has been stricken with some loathsome malady, and is not allowed to enter the dwellings of men, lays himself down, begging an alms of the passers-by by day, and by night sheltering himself among the ashes which the heat of the sun has warmed. There, too, lie the village dogs, perhaps gnawing a fallen carcass, which is often flung there.*" (From Wetzstein, quoted by Davidson and Moulton, "Modern Reader's Bible," p. 149.)

READINGS IN CHARACTER.

JOB'S WIFE (*to* JOB).

"Dost thou still hold fast thine integrity? renounce God and die."

JOB.

"Thou speakest as one of the foolish women speaketh. What? shall we receive good at the hand of God, and shall we not receive evil?"

In all this did not Job sin with his lips.

PARALLEL.—Habakkuk, a contemporary of Jeremiah, and prophesying in the last years of the kingdom of Judah, when the Chaldeans under Nebuchadnezzar were about to come and overwhelm the land, and sweep away the city, the temple, and the nation itself, sang in a hymn of prayer (iii. 17, 18):

"Though the fig-tree shall not blossom,
 Neither shall fruit be in the vines;
 The labor of the olive shall fail,
 And the fields shall yield no meat;

The flock shall be cut off from the fold,
And there shall be no herd in the stalls;
Yet will I rejoice in the Lord,
I will joy in the God of my salvation."

JOB STOOD THE TEST in this hardest kind of trial.
THE DISEASE was such as to weaken his physical power of sustaining his sufferings. Many a holy saint succumbs to despondency and doubt under diseases that affect the nerves and digestion. It is hard to make the music of hope and faith on the "harp of a thousand strings" when they are broken, and wet with tears, and out of tune. We often do not give credit enough to some persons who are struggling and fighting against disease, because they are not as joyful and triumphant as others in good health.

JOB'S WIFE is probably introduced to give the last terrible touch to the monumental suffering of Job, for now he must "tread the wine-press alone." One by one the others had failed him; his children were dead, his friends kept away, and now, at last, his wife, who had endured the other trials, yields when she sees her husband incurably diseased, and takes part against his conscience and his duty to God.

Father Taylor, the famous sailors' preacher of Boston, was greatly depressed in his last illness; and when some one tried to comfort him by the assurance that he would soon be with the angels, he replied, "I don't want angels, I want folks."

Dr. Samuel Cox is right in saying that Job's wife has been a much maligned woman, both by scholars and in the popular imagination, as if she were a kind of scriptural Xantippe. Chrysostom thought she was left alive to be a scourge of Job, the last bitter drop in his cup of suffering. It is unjust, and far from the way we would like to be judged, to infer her whole character from one sentence uttered under intense excitement. Job himself did not call her foolish, but delicately said she had uttered a foolish thing. She suffered the loss of all things, as Job did, and no murmur proceeds from her lips. The wife of such a man and the mother of such children may well be "a woman nobly planned." It must have been harder for her to see him stunned and hopeless on the ash heap than to sit there herself.

According to the story God did not judge her as harshly as men have done, for she too was raised to share his sevenfold splendors and prosperity, and to bear him sons and daughters.

ONE MORE TRIAL came later, a trial which intensified the bitter anguish of all his other calamities, in the interpretation his friends, and therefore the world, put upon his losses and sufferings. "No mortal," says Homer, "ever suffered such pain and such affliction" as his Ulysses. "The fearful dangers through which Ulysses goes exalt his fame and glorify him."

> "Ah, brother! have you not full oft
> Found even as the Romans did,
> That in life's most delicious draught
> 'Surgit amari aliquid.'"
> (Something bitter comes unbid.)

Observe that Job was enabled to stand these tests of his character because of his faithfulness in all his previous life. His faithfulness in the lesser things enabled him to be faithful in the greater things. His victories over small temptations enabled him to gain the victory in harder battles, as David by his overcoming the lion and the bear was assured that God would give him the victory over Goliath.

Search the Scriptures for teachings and examples in regard to this principle.

Observe that the character of Job, as a paragon of goodness unequalled on earth and the sufferings of Job as the utmost that can come to man, are presented in these extremes so that the instruction and comfort of the book may reach all men. God allows the worst of suffering to come upon the best of men, and Job is true to God under the most extreme of trials.

LESSONS IN THE SCHOOL OF LIFE

1. IT IS A FACT that in all ages trouble comes upon good men which cannot be explained by any connection with evil doing on their part. In some cases the trouble comes because they are good, as in the case of Job. Job was made to undergo great suffering because he was so good that his faithfulness under it would bless all generations of men to the end of the world.

> "'There is no God,' the foolish saith,
> But none, 'There is no sorrow.'"
> (Mrs. Browning, "The Cry of the Human.")

"God," says Davidson, "confers on some the high prerogative of suffering, to demonstrate to a scoffing world or an incredulous Accuser of the brethren what righteousness really means." The martyrs, prophets, apostles, Christ himself, are examples. Many more in private life.

Bring examples from observation and history where the good 'results are not so plain to the sufferer at the time.

2. NOTE THE BEARING OF THIS ON THE JUSTICE OF GOD.—In many cases we can see that men would willingly, even gladly, endure the suffering if they could see what God saw at the time, the great blessings which would come to the world through them. Christ's cross is an example.

> "They climbed the steep ascent of Heaven
> Through peril, toil and pain!
> O God, to us may grace be given
> To follow in their train."
> (Bishop Reginald Heber.)

Many of us when we get to heaven will seek first to go to the Lord and say, Forgive me, Lord, for my murmurings and complaints, and accept my inmost thanks for the way in which thou didst lead me, and the burdens thou didst lay upon me.

That cannot be unjust for which, when we understand it, we will give thanks.

3. DOES GOD SEND TROUBLE? [1]—What is the teaching of these chapters upon this question?

Trouble comes from Satan and wicked persons; as robber raids, wars, etc.

Trouble comes from the action of the laws of God, as the lightning and the storm.

The calamities of Job came by the permission of God.

But God limited and controlled the actions of evil beings.

God used the evils so as to work out good for Job and for the world.

The sufferer did not know the reasons for the troubles he endured.

But God has wise reasons for permitting them.

4. THE RELATION OF GOD TO TROUBLE.

1. **God works by law.** His laws are unchanged, inexorable. "No new laws, no changed laws, no unjust laws." They are such that obeyed they bring to man the most perfect life and character and happiness. Heaven is an example of what God's laws are enacted to produce, and will ever accomplish if men will obey them. They cannot be changed except for the worse.

A lawless universe would be the worst possible. Compare the charming story of "Hafed's Dream of a Chance World." (Todd, "Truth Made Simple." [2]) "Growth, intellectual, moral, spiritual, in every direction, means learning how to live in the midst of a universe on which you can count every time." So "God's laws for the body, obeyed, mean perfect health." (Minot J. Savage, "Pillars of the Temple.")

Mr. Richard Le Gallienne has written a book, "If I were God." Ingersoll is reported to have said that if he were God he would have made health catching instead of disease. (God has made good more catching than evil.) But we all are thankful that those authors are not God.

2. **God has given man a free will**, the power of choice, with all its possibilities of good and evil. All the evils, the wars, the crimes, the cruelties, the horrors in the history of man were made possible by this gift. But all virtue,

---

[1] See President Charles Cuthbert Hall's "Does God Send Trouble?"
[2] Published by Bridgman, Northampton, Mass., 1856.

all character, nobleness, heroism, all that makes man in the image of God, heaven itself—were also made possible by the same gift.

Some writer has imagined the Creator, when before creation he was alone in the spaces of the universe, considering whether he should create or not. He thought the question through to the end. He saw the sins and evils, devils and bad men, which would come. He saw the good, the saints, and angels, the virtues as many and as bright as the stars, the new heavens and the new earth enduring through eternal ages. And he saw it was wise and good to create.

3. **Whatsoever God does himself** is to help, to uplift, to make good, to restore, to save, to help men to conform to the good laws he has made. "God sent not the Son into the world to judge the world; but that the world should be saved through him." (John iii. 17.)

4. **God for wise reasons permits evil**—or else evil could not exist.

Evils come upon us from two sources, as they did to Job.

> Some come to us through our breaking the good laws of God, so that we suffer the natural consequences of sin. No one should complain of this.

> Some come to us through the action of God's natural laws without any connection with the character or conduct of the sufferer; as by lightning and earthquake and storm, which smite alike the good and the evil, the missionary and the pirate.

> Many come to us through the action of other beings, from inheritance, from carelessness bringing accidents and disease; from evil beings, as wars, oppressions, murders, crimes, devastations by the armies of fierce chiefs and their ravaging hordes. That Satan should be one of these evil beings is no more strange than that history should be full of mighty devastators and conquerors who have filled the world with sorrow. Satan is not only an individual, but the representative and embodiment of all evil men.

Ibsen, the Norse dramatist, " writes a drama of life which he calls 'Ghosts,' and shows how every player is haunted by dead ancestors, who look through his eyes, speak in his words, and act in his deeds."

5. **God controls and limits and uses the power of evil** men to harm—or else he would not be God. God is in history. God is guiding the nations now as really as he did Israel. A professor who conducts a Sunday-school said to me that he would rather teach his children United States history than Jewish history. The difference between them, however, is twofold. Jewish history is divinely interpreted to us, and no other history is so written; and Jewish history in the Bible is a completed section of their history, so that we can see both the processes and the results, but modern history is still in the process of making. (Compare Prof. S. H. Butcher's " Harvard Lectures on Greek Subjects," Greece and Israel, p. 43.) "Nor was it until ancient Hellas ceased to

be an independent nation that it became one of the moving forces in the world's history. With the Greeks as with the Hebrews, the days of their abasement have once and again preceded their greatest triumphs; the moment of apparent overthrow has been the starting-point for fresh spiritual or intellectual conquest." There is a true sense in which God does the strange things attributed to him in the Old Testament. Nothing is outside of his control. He says, "Moab is my washpot," by means of which to cleanse Israel. Assyria is the "rod of his anger," by which to punish Israel's sins, to make the nation better. Cyrus was his instrument of returning Israel to their own land. And always his object is to make better and to save.

6. God uses the laws of nature and is not imprisoned in them. He does not change them in order to help men, but uses them. He makes the lightning go where his laws would guide it, but he can keep you from being where it strikes.

> "When the loose mountain trembles from on high
> Shall gravitation cease if you go by?
> Or some old temple tottering to its fall
> For Chartre's head reserves the hanging wall?"

Not at all, but you may be guided not to go by, and Chartre kept from sitting at that time under the hanging wall.

All civilization is gained by man putting his will into the laws of God. He wishes a shower on his lawn? Then he puts in water-works and uses God's laws to make a shower there. He breaks no law, he changes no law. He wants better fruits and flowers, or horses, or dogs—and a Darwin or a Burbank uses God's laws to produce them.

Now it would be a strange, impossible thing that God could not do what his children can do every day. A miracle changes no law, it is simply God's putting his mighty will into his wise laws and using them. Hence, God can forgive, and modify the natural effects of the laws we have broken. He can put his hand among the laws and save a man, as naturally as a father can save his child who has become entangled in the machinery of his factory, or rescue his son from drowning, when the natural working of the laws would destroy him.

7. Therefore God, without changing a single law, can fulfil his promise, can cause that "all things shall work together for good to them that love God." We are not crushed individually under the great machinery of the universe for the general good.

"The cold and distant conception of God," says Dr. Van Dyke, "as the great onlooker,

> ' Who sees with equal eyes as God of all
> A hero perish or a sparrow fall '

is not the thought of the Bible." ("The Open Door," p. 132.)

THE FIRST SOLUTION OF THE PROBLEM

THAT TROUBLE IS SOMETIMES SENT AS A TEST OF THE REALITY OF GOODNESS

1. **To the sufferer himself.** No person can know himself till he has been tested. Even Peter did not know himself till his great test at the time of Christ's trial. Then he rejoiced in other, longer, harder tests that proved him to be true to the core. We do not sing as much as we used the hymn:

> "'Tis a point I long to know,
> Oft it causes anxious thought,
> Do I love the Lord or no,
> Am I his, or am I not?"
> (John Newton.)

It might be wise if we did feel it more. It is a point we ought to know.

Rogers, in his "Greyson Letters" (pp. 103–105), tells of a man who told him: "My conscience—a morbid one, if you will—has somehow got entangled with my nervous system, and I cannot think an evil thought without torture If I see the hungry, and feel disposed to pass them unrelieved, I seem immediately seized with pangs of hunger myself. . . . If I have any feeling of disingenuousness, that moment my too physical conscience warns me by a film over my eyes; and if I were to tell a lie, I do believe she would strike me stone blind at once. . . . And if I am tempted to vanity just now as I was when you flattered me so agreeably I feel qualms at the stomach as if I had taken an emetic. . . . How I sigh for the power to do any one good thing unconstrained! —and, alas, how shall I ever be sure that I am in a condition of confirmed virtue while necessity thus backs conscience."

Plato, in his "Republic," uses as an illustration the story of Gyges' Ring to show what is the real test of goodness. The story is that a certain Lydian shepherd (about 600 B.C.) found in some strange way a gold ring. Coming with this ring on his finger into the meeting of the shepherds making their monthly report of their flocks to the king, "he happened to turn the stone of the ring toward himself into the inner part of his hand; and when this was done he became invisible to those who sat beside him, and they talked of him as absent; and astonished at this he again handled his ring, turned the stone outward, and on turning it, became visible." He made trial of this several times, and found that it always had the same power. Using this power of invisibility, he entered the palace, slew the king, and took possession of the queen and of the kingdom. This shepherd thought he was a very good man, but the ring tested the reality of his goodness. A truly just man would be just even when no one would know his wrongs if he committed them. The man who was only seemingly and outwardly just, would commit crimes if he could do it without discovery. I can know whether I am good, or wise or honest, or loving, or truthful, only after I have been tempted and tried.

Learn Xavier's hymn:

> "My God, I love thee, not because
> I hope for heaven thereby;
> Nor yet because if I love not
> I must forever die.

> "Not with the hope of gaining aught,
> Not seeking a reward,
> But as thyself hast loved me,
> O ever-loving Lord."

2. A Test for others. There is a tendency to join in Satan's sneers at the reality of goodness. It forms an excuse for themselves not being good. As Glory McWhirk said, "Anybody can be good on five thousand a year." Of all the sermons I heard in my college days the best remembered sentence is the statement made by one of the professors that whenever any one said that all men are dishonest we could be sure of one thing, that he was dishonest, for he knew himself, however little he knew of others.

One does not know whether another has courage till that courage is tested. (See article on Courage in the *Century Magazine* for June, 1888, quoted in part in Peloubet's "Suggestive Illustrations on Matthew," pp. 224, 225.)

Christ's victory over temptation, and his going to the cross, were proofs to the world of his heroism and love.

Dwight L. Moody was accused, in my presence, of doing his evangelizing work for money. But I knew that he and Mr. Sankey had refused to accept for themselves the copyright on their singing books, amounting to several hundred thousand dollars, as rightfully theirs as any money ever earned, lest any one should think they were working for money.

It was thought at one time that the Chinese converts were seeking chiefly "the loaves and fishes," but when the Boxer uprising came they stood the test and died rather than renounce God and Christ.

One of the most difficult things in the world is rightly to judge another. George William Curtis in his "Prue and I" represents Mr. Titbottom with a pair of spectacles of such magical quality that with them he saw through all appearances into the real character of the person he was looking at. He looked at one man and saw nothing but a ledger. Another was simply a billiard cue, another a bank bill, another a great hog, or a wolf, or a vulgar fraction. On the other hand, he saw the good that others failed to see. One of his school teachers was a deep well of living water in which he saw the stars. Another was a tropical garden full of fruits and flowers. In one woman's heart lay concealed in the depth of character great excellences like pearls at the bottom of the sea, little suspected by most, but perhaps love is nothing else than the sight of them by one person. Another, called an old maid, was a white lily, fresh, luminous, and fragrant still. Another's nature was a tropic in which the sun shone, and birds sang, and flowers bloomed forever. His wrinkled grandmother appeared as a Madonna, "and I have yet heard of no queen, no belle, no imperial beauty whom in grace, and brilliancy, and persuasive courtesy she might not have surpassed." The way a man meets temptation, and endures trials, shows the world what sort of a man he is, the quality of his piety, the reality of his virtue.

Search the Scriptures for examples, such as Abraham, Noah, Moses, and the list of heroes in Hebrews xi.

In John ix we learn that the blind man of Jerusalem was born blind not on account of any sin of his own or of his parents, "but that the works of God should be made manifest in him." The work of God in healing him has been shining down nineteen centuries. Helen Keller is a similar instance of God's marvellous work. So Job by his sufferings has showed forth God's glory to the world.

PART II

A DISCUSSION BETWEEN JOB AND HIS THREE FRIENDS ON THE PROBLEM OF HIS SUFFERING. POETRY. (Chapters iii–xxxi.)

THREE CYCLES OF SPEECHES

SOLUTION: SOMETIMES SUFFERING IS A CONSEQUENCE AND PUNISHMENT OF SIN. BUT IT IS NOT FOR US TO JUDGE OTHERS

RESEARCH QUESTIONS

(To be assigned to different members of the class the previous lesson; and for class discussion.)

1. Brief review of Part I.
2. Geography. The place from which the three friends came, and the distances travelled.
3. The character of Eliphaz.
4. The character of Bildad.
5. The character of Zophar.
6. The scene. The condition and circumstances of Job as gathered from his speeches.
7. The patience of Job. Does his cursing the day of his birth show that he was impatient?
8. Why were the friends silent for seven days? The lesson this teaches as to comforting others.
9. What was the argument of the three friends?
10. Why cannot we judge of another's character by his sufferings?
11. The bearing of Luke xiii. 1–5 on the problem.
12. Were the friends right in defending the justice of God? Wherein were they wrong?
13. Give a summary of Job's reply.
14. When is affliction a natural consequence of sin?
15. A study of Old Testament teachings as to the relation of sin and suffering.
16. A study of the New Testament teachings on this subject.

PLAN OF THE DISCUSSION

Silence, 7 days

JOB'S Lamentation.   Chapter iii

First Cycle	Eliphaz	Chapters	iv, v
	Job	"	vi, vii
	Bildad	"	viii
	Job	"	ix, x
	Zophar	"	xi
	Job	"	xii, xiii, xiv

Second Cycle	Eliphaz	Chapters	xv
	Job	"	xvi, xvii
	Bildad	"	xviii
	Job	"	xix
	Zophar	"	xx
	Job	"	xxi

Third Cycle	Eliphaz	Chapters	xxii
	Job	"	xxiii, xxiv
	Bildad	"	xxv
	Job	"	xxvi–xxviii
Job's Review of his Life		"	xxix, xxx
Job's Oath of Clearance		"	xxxi

Moulton's rearrangement of third cycle

Third Cycle	Eliphaz	Chapters	xxii
	Job	"	xxiii, xxiv
	Bildad	"	xxv, xxvi. 4–10
	Job	"	xxvi. 1–3; xxvii. 1–6
	Zophar	"	xxvii. 7–xxviii. 28
	Job	"	xxix, xxx
Job's Oath of Clearance		"	xxxi

THE SCENE [1]

On the city ash heap[2] outside the walls of Uz, JOB *is sitting apart, groaning and sighing with pain, covered with boils, scraping himself with a piece of broken pottery to alleviate the intolerable itching, disfigured so that his friends could not recognize him.*

He loathed his own life. His disease clung to him like a garment, so that his very clothes loathed him. His bones burned with fever. They clung to his skin. He had become a skeleton, a brother of jackals. His roarings poured out like water. The terrors of God set in array against him like a hostile army haunted his weary nights, as he tossed to and fro through the long restless hours.

His brothers, his familiar friends, his neighbors, kept far away and forgot him. The boys despised him. His enemies gaped at him. His servants refused to obey him. He was mocked by the children of those so base that in his prosperity he would have scourged them out of the land. Ragamuffins whose fathers he would have deemed unworthy to keep company with his dogs made him their song and byword.

He was a poor, prematurely old man, a failure, seemingly under the curse of God, stripped of his glory, and seeing nothing before him but the land of darkness and the shadow of death.

Compare Prometheus nailed to a great rock with an eagle continually gnawing at his vitals. (See "Æschylus" in "Ancient Classics for English Readers," pp. 33–62.)

Compare also Christian in the dungeon of the castle of Giant Despair; but Job was without Hopeful and the Key of Promise.

HISTORICAL EXAMPLES.—"A man like Dante or Milton," says Farrar, "when he stands alone, hated by princes and priests and people, retorts scorn for scorn, and refuses to change his voice. Yet even Dante died of a broken heart, and in Milton's mighty autobiographical wail of Samson Agonistes, amid all its trumpet-blast of stern defiance, we read the sad notes:

> 'Nor am I in the list of them that hope;
> Hopeless are all my evils, all remediless,
> This one prayer yet remains, might I be heard,
> No long petition—speedy death,
> The close of all my miseries and the balm.'"

THE COMING OF THE THREE FRIENDLY CHIEFS.—The news of Job's misfortune came to the ears of three chiefs, all men of mark, who were friends

---

[1] This description is gathered from Job's own words in his speeches, with one or two statements in the introduction. See Job ii. 7, 8; iii. 21, 22, 26; vi. 2–4; vii. 4, 5, 16; ix. 30, 31; x. 20–22; xvi. 8–10, 16; xvii. 2, 6, 14; xix. 9, 13–18, 20, 21; xxx. 1, 9, 10, 15, 17–19, 23, 29–31. It is a good exercise to go through Job's speeches to learn what he says of himself.

[2] For description of ash heap, see page 11.

of Job, and they started from their distant homes to bemoan and comfort their afflicted friend. They probably came on camels and with something of a retinue and met at Uz by an appointment together.

Eliphaz came from Teman, in Edom, the home of the descendants of Esau, near the southern part of the Dead Sea, perhaps one hundred and fifty to two hundred miles southwest of Uz.

Bildad came from Shuah, east of Uz, toward the Euphrates, perhaps as far away as Eliphaz.

Zophar came from Naamah, perhaps Maan near Petra, sixty miles south of the Dead Sea, half way between the Dead Sea and the eastern branch of the Red Sea. He would naturally pass through Teman on his way.

"Probably they were all three of them nomadic princes, the sheiks of wandering clans, with whom Job had become acquainted in his travels, or in his large and varied intercourse with the world." (Cox, "Commentary on Job," p. 57.)

"From their meeting-place at Teman or at Maan, they would have to make a journey of some two hundred miles across one of the most barren and dangerous deserts of Arabia—clear enough proof of their esteem for Job, and their deep sympathy." (Marcus Dods, D.D., "Expositor's Bible," p. 79.)

THEIR MEETING WITH JOB. (Job ii. 11–13.)

They did not recognize Job when they saw him, so disfigured and unnatural did he appear. They expressed their grief in the usual Oriental manner, by weeping aloud,[1] rending their clothes,[2] and sprinkling ashes upon their heads.[3] Then for seven days and seven nights they were silent, not a word was spoken, "for they saw that his grief was very great."

THE SEVEN DAYS OF SILENCE.—This is one of the finest touches in the poem. The long silence indicates the true gentleman with fine courtesy and true feeling. Words are vain to comfort in the depths of affliction.

> "And my comforter knows a lesson
> Wiser, truer than the rest:
> That to help and heal a sorrow
> Love and silence are always best."
> (Miss Proctor, "The Comforter.")

So Tennyson:

> "Only silence suiteth best.
> Words, weaker than your grief, would make
> Grief more. 'Twere better I should cease."
> (To J. S.)

---

[1] Cries and laments: 2 Sam. i. 17–27; iii. 33, 34; xviii. 33; 2 Kin. ii. 12; 2 Chron. xxxv. 25.

[2] Mourners rending their garments: Gen. xxxvii. 29, 34; xliv. 13; Num. xiv. 6; Jud. xi. 35; 2 Sam. i. 2, 4; iii. 31; xiii. 19, 31; xv. 32; 2 Kin. ii. 12; v. 8; vi. 30; xi. 14; xix. 1; xxii. 11, 19; Ezra ix. 3, 5; Jer. xli. 5; Matt. xxvi. 65; Acts xiv. 14.

[3] Ashes and dust in mourning: Josh. vii. 6; 2 Sam. xiii. 19; 1 Kin. xx. 38; Esth. iv. 1; Rev. xviii. 19.

"Wise-hearted was Southey's young Arabian, in watching silently the frantic grief of the newly childless old divine: in pitying silence Thalaba stood by, and gazed and listened: 'not with the officious hand of consolation, fretting the sore he could not hope to heal.'" (Jacox. His "Secular Annotations" gives a number of instances from literature.)

> "Seven days and nights, in stillness as profound
> As that of chaos, patiently ye sate
> By the heart-stricken and the desolate.
> And though your sympathy might fail to sound
> The fathomless depths of his dark spirit's wound,
> Not less your silence was sublimely great."
> (Anon. in "Poet's Bible.")

THE GREAT DEBATE

CHARACTERISTICS OF THE CHIEF SPEAKERS [1]

JOB has been characterized on page 4.

ELIPHAZ was the oldest and wisest of the three. An Abraham-like saint, of a dignified and noble character, rather than brilliant or learned; "with a considerable likeness to Job himself in the general cast of his character and his tone of thought." Firm in his opinions; of plain common sense. He gives by far the noblest, gentlest, and most artistic expressions of the convictions and sentiments common to all. "He has been brought into closer and more intimate intercourse with heaven than his fellows, and like Balaam, another son of the ancient East, is a seer of visions and a dreamer of dreams." (See Cox, "Commentary on Job," p. 55.)

Cary calls him a Venerable Theologian, and a Deep Thinker.

BILDAD was a sage, a man of literary culture, a treasure-house of the priceless wisdom of the ancients. He quotes the proverbs of the sages, and bases his opinions on the traditions of the fathers, whom he frequently cites.

Cary calls him a Traditionalist.

ZOPHAR was the ordinary good man of his day, with a commonplace mind, savoring of bigotry, and uttering common thoughts in a commonplace manner. "The man who implicitly believes what he is taught, and demands not only that every one else should believe it, but in the very forms which commended the truth to him."

"He is sharp and bitter . . . he put a coarse tearing edge on the insinuations of his companions; and prided himself, I dare say, on being a plain, blunt man who said what he meant, and meant what he said." He calls Job "a windbag," "a babbler," "an empty pate," "a wild ass's colt."

[1] Derived from the words of the speakers themselves. It is a good exercise for each scholar to make such a study for himself.

"Having no familiar acquaintance with the voice of wisdom, no divine vision to fall back upon, he delivers his commonplace opinions with an air of authority. He has a touch of 'I am Sir Oracle, let no dog bark.'" (See Froude, "Essay on Job," and Cox, "Commentary on Job," p. 55.)

THE AUDIENCE *consisted of* ELIHU, *the brothers and kinsmen of* JOB, *neighbors, citizens, curiosity-mongers, servants, children, visitors.*

Unseen, but present, were GOD, *angels, and* "*a great cloud of witnesses*" *interested in the test. And the* ADVERSARY *watching the result of his endeavors to make* JOB *fail.*

READINGS IN CHARACTER.

Selections from each speaker giving the gist of the argument and the passages of special note.

The whole discussion should be read at home.

All the selections given below from the Great Debate should be read at one time in the class.

JOB'S LAMENTATION. (Chapter iii.)

JOB.

"Let the day perish wherein I was born.

Let that day be darkness;
Let not God regard it from above,
Neither let the light shine upon it!
Let darkness and the shadow of death claim it for their
    own;
Let a cloud dwell upon it;
Let all that maketh black the day terrify it!
Let the stars of the twilight thereof be dark!
Let it look for light, but have none;
Neither let it behold the eyelids of the morning.
Why died I not from the womb?
For now should I have lien down and been quiet;
I should have slept; then had I been at rest:
    With kings and counsellors of the earth.
There the wicked cease from troubling;
And there the weary be at rest.

> Wherefore is light given to him that is in misery,
> And life unto the bitter in soul;
> Which long for death, but it cometh not;
> And dig for it more than for hid treasures.
> For the thing which I fear cometh upon me,
> And that which I am afraid of cometh unto me." [1]

"Curse" in verse 1 is not the same word which Job's wife uses in A. V., where she bids Job to "curse," i. e., "renounce" God and die.

Compare Shakespeare's "King Richard," exclaiming:

> "My large kingdom for a little grave,
> A little, little grave, an obscure grave."
> ("King Richard II," Act iii, Sc. 3.)

The first eighteen sections of Tennyson's "In Memoriam" are strikingly parallel to Job's Lament in this chapter and to his first answer to Eliphaz, chapters vi, vii.

Sophocles in "Œdipus Colonnus" expresses "in sharpest form the ruling thought of the first two strophes of Job's curse."

Shakespeare in one of his finest passages seems to have had this chapter in his eye, as in "King John" (Act. iii, Sc. 1), the speech of Constance beginning "A wicked day and not a holy day," and in a later passage (Act iii, Sc. 4), "O amiable and lovely death!" etc.

"The eyelids of the morning" (iii. 9). A beautiful picture. The morning rays streaming through the opening clouds seem "like the light of the eyes of day pouring through its opening lids and lashes." Sophocles ("Antigone," 103) speaks of "the eyelid of the golden day." Milton ("Lycidas," 26) speaks of "the opening eyelids of the morn."

"The thing which I feared is come upon me" (iii. 25). The element of fear (not fear of God, but of future evil, anxiety) seems to have been too large an element in his piety, and it was intensified by his disease. "Gloomy and terrifying apprehensions are one of the most painful symptoms of Elephantiasis. Genung says that one important result of Job's trial will be to change his piety from negative to positive, from fear to love." ("Epic of the Inner Life," p. 150.)

"A curious illustration . . . occurs in Dean Swift's writings. Swift's melancholy habit of 'lamenting his birthday' by reading the third chapter of Job is familiar to all interested in his life." (Bradley, "Lecture on Job," p. 19.)

THE PATIENCE OF JOB.—A number of the writers on Job speak as if Job lost his patience in this discussion; that is, at the time when his patience was

---

[1] Job iii. 3–5, 9, 11, 13, 14, 17, 20, 21, 25.

most severely tried. But it is these very expressions of deep feeling which prove his patience. If he had been a marble statue or a being "carved in ice"; if he were sitting "like patience on a monument, smiling at grief," he would have shown no strong feeling about his wrongs, for he would have had none. But it does not require patience in such a being to keep from complaining. Job was fighting a terrible battle, but he held on till he gained the victory. His complaints prove the intensity of his feelings; and yet he never lost his faith, never yielded to the tempter. That is patience. Just as courage is not indifference to danger, nor ignorance of it, but a going straightforward in the path of duty when the greatness of the danger is so realized as to blanch the cheeks, and almost stop the beating of the heart. Two soldiers were charging up a hill with their regiment, in a desperate attempt to capture a battery. "When half way up, one of them turned to the other, and said, 'Why, you are as pale as a sheet; you look like a ghost; I believe you are afraid.' 'Yes, I am,' was the answer; 'and, if you were half as much afraid as I am, you'd have run long ago.'" Some one reported to Napoleon that one of his officers turned pale when ordered to a dangerous duty. "That officer," replied Napoleon, "is one of the bravest in the whole army; he sees most clearly the danger, but will do his duty in spite of it." (See *Century Magazine* for June, 1888.)

Mr. Howard in his life of Henry Clay Trumbull tells how as chaplain he so dreaded the first battle that he turned to his servant and said: "If you see me turning back, shoot me." No man was braver. Often the timid, who dread the smallest things, are far more courageous than those who physically have no thought of fear. In my first parish at Gloucester, my wife and I went out in a wherry after a storm. The fishermen said we did not know enough to be afraid.

These illustrations apply equally to patience. Many a person of shattered nerves, weakened by depressing disease, who is fretful and impatient, may be really far more patient than the well persons who criticise him.[1]

> "'Tis all men's office to speak patience
> To those writhing under the bond of sorrow;
> But no man's virtue, nor sufficiency,
> To be so moral when he shall endure
> The like himself."
> ("Much Ado About Nothing," Act v, Sc. 1.)

[1] Compare Christ's word from the cross, "My God, my God, why hast thou forsaken me?" (Matt. xxvii. 46); David's grief over Absalom (2 Sam. xviii. 33); Psalm cxxx, "Out of the depths have I cried unto thee."

THE FIRST CYCLE OF SPEECHES. (Chapters iv–xiv.)

ELIPHAZ (chapters iv, v).

If one essay to commune with thee, wilt thou be grieved?
But who can withhold himself from speaking?
  Behold, thou hast instructed many,
  And thou hast strengthened the weak hands.
  Thy words have upholden him that was falling,
  And thou hast confirmed the feeble knees.
  But now it is come unto thee, and thou faintest;
  It toucheth thee, and thou art troubled.

Remember, I pray thee, who ever perished, being innocent?
  Or where were the upright cut off?

According as I have seen, they that plow iniquity,
And sow trouble, reap the same.
  By the breath of God they perish,
  And by the blast of his anger are they consumed.

  In thoughts from the visions of the night,
  When deep sleep falleth on men,
  Fear came upon me and trembling,
  Which made all my bones to shake.
  Then a spirit passed before my face;
  The hair of my flesh stood up.
  It stood still, but I could not discern the appearance thereof;
  A form was before mine eyes:
  There was silence, and I heard a voice, saying,
"Shall mortal man be more just than God?
Shall a man be more pure than his Maker?"

For affliction cometh not forth of the dust,
  Neither doth trouble spring out of the ground;
  But man is born unto trouble,
As the sparks fly upward.

But as for me, I would seek unto God,
And unto God would I commit my cause.
Behold, happy is the man whom God correcteth: [1]
Therefore despise not thou the chastening of the Almighty.
For he maketh sore, and bindeth up;
He woundeth, and his hands make whole.

He shall deliver thee in six troubles;
Yea, in seven there shall no evil touch thee.
Lo this, we have searched it, so it is;
Hear it, and know thou it for thy good. [2]

Compare Milton's description of death (in "Paradise Lost," ii. 266):

"If shape it could be called that shape had none
Distinguishable in member, joint or limb;
Or substance might be called that shadow seemed."

Job iv. 17 is not a mere truism, as some say, but contains the gist of his argument—a good man would not inflict punishment on one who had done right. Much more is such injustice impossible with God. Therefore, Job must have done some great wrong. The flaw in his argument is that he takes for granted that all suffering is a punishment, which the Prologue, as we have seen, shows to be a false assumption. This false argument Eliphaz states in several ways in this speech—either God is unjust, and therefore not God, or Job is a sinner.

JOB (chapters vi, vii).

Oh that my vexation were but weighed,
And my calamity laid in the balances together!
For now it would be heavier than the sand of the seas:
Therefore have my words been rash.

To him that is ready to faint
Kindness should be shewed from his friend;
Even to him that forsaketh the fear of the Almighty.

[1] See Ps. xciv. 12; cvii; Heb. xii. 5–11.
[2] Job iv. 1–5, 7–9, 13, 17; v. 6–8, 17–19, 27. See Byron, "Hebrew Melodies;" From Job.

My brethren have dealt deceitfully as a brook,
As the channel of brooks that pass away.
Did I say, "Give unto me?"[1]
Or, "Offer a present for me of your substance?"
Or, "Deliver me from the adversary's hand?"
Or, "Redeem me from the hand of the oppressors?"

Teach me and I will hold my peace;
    And cause me to understand wherein I have erred.
How forcible are words of uprightness!
    But what doth your arguing reprove?
Yea, ye would cast lots upon the fatherless,
And make merchandise of your friend.

(The FRIENDS, *vexed at the reproof, rise
and consult together.)*[2]

Now therefore be pleased to look upon me;
    For surely I shall not lie to your face.

(The FRIENDS *are turning to go away.)*[2]

Return, I pray you, let there be no injustice.

(The FRIENDS *sit down again.)*[2]

Is there not a warfare[3] to man upon earth?
Are not his days like the days of an hireling?
    As a servant that earnestly desireth the shadow,[4]
    The night is long;
And I am full of tossing to and fro unto the dawning of the day.
    My days are swifter than a weaver's shuttle,
    And are spent without hope.
As the cloud is consumed and vanisheth away.

[1] Did I ask you to come and help me? Why then come as if you were my friends, and then disappoint me so?

[2] These italics are from Cary. Renan suggests the same thought, that, stung by the irony and keen reproaches of Job, the friends make a movement to retire.

[3] Margin, "a time of service."

[4] Shadow on the sun dial, showing that the day is ending.

(*To* God.)

Am I a sea or a sea-monster,
That thou settest a watch over me?
Then thou scarest me with dreams,
And terrifiest me through visions:
So that my soul chooseth strangling,
And death rather than these my bones.
I loathe my life;
I would not live alway;
Let me alone;
For my days are vanity.

What is man, that thou shouldest magnify him,
And that thou shouldest set thine heart upon him,
And that thou shouldest visit him every morning?[1]

The Oriental brooks running through the rocky ravines become suddenly torrents after a rain, because there are no forests to hold the water back. In the hot, dry season, the bed of the brook is dry, when the thirsty traveller is most in need of water. So swiftly, so disappointingly disappeared the human sympathy and love Job longed for. "O the pity of it, the pity of it!"

I have heard Henry Ward Beecher during his great trial in one of his prayer meetings define his position by an experience of his in the exciting antislavery times. He with another speaker were mobbed at a meeting in the city. They escaped by a back exit, but were followed by the mob. He entered a certain house, but the mob thought he was in the house opposite, which they attacked with stones, rotten eggs and every kind of missile. All this time Mr. Beecher was calmly looking on from his safe retreat. "It did not harm me," he said, "for I was not there."

Job was deprived of sleep

"That knits up the ravel'd sleave of care,
The death of each day's life, sore labor's bath,
Balm of hurt minds."
("Macbeth," Act ii, Sc. 1.)

"A sea, or a sea-monster" (vii, 12). The sea itself is sometimes likened to one of its monsters "twisting about the land and at times invading and destroy-

[1] Job vi. 2, 3, 14, 15, 22, 25, 27-29; vii. 1, 2, 4, 6, 9, 12, 14-18. For a parallel to this pathetic description of life, see Deut. xxviii. 65-67.

ing" and requiring transcendent power to tame and restrain it with God's "Hitherto shalt thou come. and no further, and here shall thy proud waves be stayed." (Job xxxviii. 11.)

The "sea-monster" was the untamable crocodile, or one of those monstrous

> "dragons of the prime
> That tare each other in their slime."

Job complains "that he, a man, 'noble in reason, infinite in faculty,'" with a conscience and heart, "should be handled roughly and severely as though like sea or monster he were devoid of sense and reason." (Cox, "Commentary on Job," p. 108.)

Contrast Job vii. 17 with Ps. viii. 3, 4, one of the older Psalms. As if God instead of being mindful of man and visiting him in order to help and comfort and save, visited him every morning to test and try him. So Stead in his "If Christ Came to Chicago," represents Christ as searching for all kinds of evil, but looking for very little good.

BILDAD (chapter viii).

How long wilt thou speak these things?
And how long shall the words of thy mouth be like a mighty wind?

Doth God pervert judgment?
Or doth the Almighty pervert justice?
If thy children have sinned against him,
And he have delivered them into the hand of their transgression:
    If thou wouldest seek diligently unto God,
    And make thy supplication to the Almighty;
    If thou wert pure and upright;
Surely now he would awake for thee,
And make the habitation of thy righteousness prosperous.

For inquire, I pray thee, of the former age,
And apply thyself to that which their fathers have searched out:
(For we are but of yesterday, and know nothing).

Can the flag grow without water?
    Whilst it is yet in its greenness, and not cut down,
    It withereth before any other herb.
So are the paths of all that forget God;
And the hope of the godless man shall perish:

Behold, God will not cast away a perfect man,
Neither will he uphold the evil-doers.[1]

In Bildad's speech the doctrine of Eliphaz is reasserted with more heat and based upon appeals to nature and tradition.

Bildad appeals to three proverbs: (1) that of the "Reed and the Rush," vs. 11–13; (2) of "the Spider's Web," vs. 14, 15; (3) of "the Gourd," vs. 16–18. (see Cox, "Commentary on Job," pp. 114–116.)

JOB (chapters ix, x).
Of a truth I know that it is so:
But how can man be just with God?

If he be pleased to contend with him
He cannnot answer him one of a thousand.
Who hath hardened himself against him and prospered?
Which removeth the mountains and they know it not,
Which alone stretcheth out the heavens,
And treadeth upon the waves of the sea.
Which maketh the Bear, Orion, and the Pleiades,
And the chambers of the south.
Which doeth great things past finding out;
Yea, marvellous things without number.

If I say, "I will forget my complaint,
I will put off my sad countenance,
And be of good cheer:"
I am afraid of all my sorrows,
I know that thou wilt not hold me innocent,
I shall be condemned.
If I wash myself with snow water,
And make my hands never so clean;
Yet wilt thou plunge me in the ditch,
And mine own clothes shall abhor me.
For he is not a man as I am, that I should answer him.
There is no daysman betwixt us.

[1] Job viii. 2–6, 8, 9, 11–13, 20.

That might lay his hand upon us both.
Then would I speak and not fear him.

(*To* GOD.)

If I sin,
Then thou markest me,
  If I be wicked,
  Woe unto me;
  And if I be righteous,
  Yet shall I not lift up my head.
Thou huntest me as a lion.[1]

(*To the* FRIENDS.)

Are not my days few? Cease then,
And let me alone, that I may take comfort a little,
Before I go whence I shall not return,
Even to the land of darkness and of the shadow of death.[2]

"Bear, Orion, Pleiades" (ix. 9) are the modern names of these constellations, which with one exception are the same as Vulcan wrought upon the disk of the massy shield which the goddess Thetis had begged for her son Achilles. (See Homer's "Iliad," xviii. 486–89.)

"Chambers of the south" (ix. 9), the storehouses of the rain; or "the vast starry groups of the southern hemisphere." (Cox, "Commentary on Job," p. 123.)

"Wash myself with snow water" (ix. 30); compare Ps. li. 7: "Wash me and I shall be whiter than snow," and the exquisite poem "Beautiful Snow,"[3] beginning "Oh the snow! the beautiful snow!"

"Once I was pure as the snow, but I fell,
  Fell like the snowflake, from heaven to hell;
  Fell to be trampled as filth in the street;
  Fell to be scoffed at, derided, and beat.
    Pleading,
        Cursing,
                Dreading to die,
  Selling my soul to whoever would buy.

[1] As a lion hunts for his prey.

[2] Job ix. 2–5, 8–10, 27–33, 35; x. 14–16, 20, 21. See clear description of Sheol among early Hebrew beliefs in Professor Orr's "Christian View of God and His World," Appendix to Lecture V.

[3] In "Snowflakes," p. 69 (Am. Tract Soc.), quoted largely in Pelouhet's "Suggestive Illustrations on Acts," p. 334. (Holman.)

Merciful God! have I fallen so low?
And yet I was once like the beautiful snow
Father, mother, sisters, all—
God and myself I have lost by my fall.
.　.　.　.　.　.　.
Helpless and foul as the trampled snow,
Sinner, despair not!　Christ stoopeth low
To rescue the soul that is lost in its sin,
And raise it to life and enjoyment again.
　　Groaning,
　　　　Bleeding,
　　　　　　Dying for thee,
The crucified hung on the accursed tree.
His accents of pity fall soft on thine ear.
'Is there mercy for me?　Will He heed my weak prayer?
O God, in the stream that for sinners did flow,
Wash me, and I shall be whiter than snow!'"

In Lockman's Fable the black man rubs his body with snow in order to make it white.

"A daysman" (ix. 33), a mediator, an umpire (so named as having the appointment of a day for hearing the cause). Here is expressed the human need of a Saviour who should be both God and man. "Job, like Plato, was profoundly sure that he should never know God as he needed to know Him until some man or spirit was sent to reveal God to his longing soul." Again in xvi. 19, he feels more sure of the advocate; and in xix. 25, he can say "I know that my Redeemer liveth."

ZOPHAR (chapter xi).
Should not the multitude of words be answered?
And should a man full of talk be justified?
Should thy boastings make men hold their peace?
　But Oh that God would speak,
　And open his lips against thee;
Know therefore that God exacteth of thee
Less than thine iniquity deserveth.

Canst thou by searching find out God?
Canst thou find out the Almighty unto perfection?
　It is high as heaven; what canst thou do?
　Deeper than Sheol; what canst thou know?

The measure thereof is longer than the earth,
And broader than the sea.
If iniquity be in thine hand, put it far away,
And let not unrighteousness dwell in thy tent,
And thy life shall be clearer than the noonday;
Though there be darkness, it shall be as the morning.
But the eyes of the wicked shall fail,
And they shall have no way to flee,
And their hope shall be the giving up of the ghost.[1]

JOB (chapters xii–xiv).

No doubt but ye are the people,
And wisdom shall die with you.

But I have understanding as well as you;
I am not inferior to you:
Yea, who knoweth not such things as these?

But ask now the beasts, and they shall teach thee;
And the fowls of the air, and they shall tell thee;
Or, speak to the earth, and it shall teach thee;
And the fishes of the sea shall declare unto thee.
Who knoweth not in all these
That the hand of the Lord hath wrought this?
In whose hand is the soul of every living thing,
And the breath of all mankind.

Surely I would speak to the Almighty,
And I desire to reason with God.
But ye are forgers of lies,
Ye are all physicians of no value.
Oh that ye would altogether hold your peace!
And it should be your wisdom.

Man that is born of a woman
Is of few days and full of trouble.

[1] Job xi. 1, 2, 3, 5, 7–9, 14, 17, 20

He cometh forth like a flower, and is cut down.
He fleeth also as a shadow and continueth not.

For there is hope of a tree, if it be cut down,
That it will sprout again.

Though the root thereof wax old in the earth,
And the stock thereof die in the ground;
Yet through the scent of water it will bud,
And put forth boughs, like a plant.
 But man dieth, and wasteth away:
 Yea, man giveth up the ghost, and where is he?
 As the waters fail from the sea,
 And the river decayeth and drieth up;
So man lieth down and riseth not;
Till the heavens be no more they shall not awake,
Nor be roused out of their sleep.

——If a man die, shall he live again?——
All the days of my warfare would I wait, till my release should
 come.[1]

The only time that the name Jehovah occurs in the poetical part of the book
is in verse 9 of chapter xii. There may be a reference to Job's words when he
was told of the death of his children. (Job i. 21.)

"Warfare" (xii. 14) means rather "a time of service," as of a soldier in
the hard toil of the campaign waiting for the time appointed for his discharge.

Job's thoughts take, in verse 7 of chapter xiv, a more hopeful turn: "Man
die while even trees live on? Impossible!" So Job speaks out his yearning
and his hope. We have here a picture of faith struggling for a revelation from
the unseen Beyond. Compare Tennyson's "In Memoriam," xliii: "If sleep
and death be truly one," etc.

THE RESULTANT OF THE FIRST ROUND OF THE DEBATE

1. Job won a logical victory over the Friends. They had little to urge except
that the Heavens are just, "and of our pleasant vices make instruments to
plague us." But Job was conscious that he was innocent of the secret vices
with which they charged him.

[1] Job xii. 2, 3, 7-10; xiii. 3-5; xiv. 1, 2, 7-12, 14.

2. He had refuted and conquered the great Adversary, Satan, the Accuser. He had not renounced God. He was enabled to trust God and preserve his allegiance to him. Othello finely complains (Act iv, Sc. 2):

> "Had it pleased Heaven
> To try me with affliction; had he rained
> All kinds of sores and shames on my bare head,
> Steeped me in poverty to the very lips,
> Given to captivity me and my utmost hopes;
> I should have found in some place of my soul
> A drop of patience; but, alas, to make me
> The fixed figure of the time for scorn
> To point his slow and moving finger at!
> Yet could I bear that too; well, very well."

Job had borne both trials which Othello affirms that he could have borne with patience. So far from renouncing God who no longer loaded him with benefits, he was led by his very deprivations and miseries to a clearer knowledge of him, a more assured and triumphant faith in him.

3. Besides his victory over the Friends, and his far greater victory over the Adversary, Job carries off, as the spoils of victory, at least an inkling or two of the greatest truths even now revealed to man—a presentiment both of the Incarnation and of the Resurrection from the dead.

Compare Wordsworth's experience, as given in his poem:

> 'And when the stream
> Which overflowed the soul was passed away,
> A consciousness remained that it had left,
> Deposited upon the silent shore
> Of memory, images and precious thoughts
> That shall not die, and cannot be destroyed."

("Excursion," Bk. vii.)   (From Cox, "Commentary on Job," pp. 177–80.)

THE SECOND CYCLE OF SPEECHES

It is probable that an interval of time lies between the different cycles of speaking, a time for meditation, and settling of opinions. But there is no change in the argument, except more intense and passionate utterances, and a firmer conviction on the part of each one that he is right, while JOB *grows more calm and self-possessed.*

THE SCENE *is the same as before.*

THE STARTING POINT *is the claim on both sides of a pre-eminent acquaintance with Divine Wisdom.*

ELIPHAZ (chapter xv).

Should a wise man make answer with vain knowledge,
     And fill his belly with the east wind?
Should he reason with unprofitable talk,
     Or with speeches wherewith he can do no good?
Thine own mouth condemneth thee, and not I;
     Yea, thine own lips testify against thee.

Art thou the first man that was born?
     Or wast thou brought forth before the hills?
Hast thou heard the secret counsel of God?
     And dost thou restrain wisdom to thyself?
What knowest thou, that we know not?

Are the consolations of God too small for thee?

What is man,
     That he should be clean?
And he which is born of a woman,
     That he should be righteous?
Behold, he putteth no trust in his holy ones;
Yea, the heavens are not clean in his sight.
How much less one that is abominable and corrupt,
A man that drinketh iniquity like water!

39

I will shew thee, hear thou me;
And that which I have seen I will declare:
  (Which wise men have told
  From their fathers.)

The wicked man travaileth with pain all his days,
Even the number of years that are laid up for the oppressor.
A sound of terrors is in his ears;
In prosperity the spoiler shall come upon him:
Distress and anguish make him afraid.
Because he hath stretched out his hand against God,
And behaveth himself proudly against the Almighty;
He runneth upon him with a stiff neck,
  With the thick bosses of his bucklers.
He shall shake off his unripe grape as the vine,
And shall cast off his flower as the olive.[1]

"A wise man" (xv. 2). Eliphaz was older than Job, came from Teman, a place noted for its wisdom, and, "evidently prides himself on belonging to the guild of wise men."

"East wind" (xv. 2). "Puff himself up, and then bring out of his mouth violent blasts of mere barren words" (Hos. xii. 1). ("Cambridge Bible," p. 109.)

"The first man" (xv. 7), and therefore summing up all the wisdom of the world. Compare the ironical proverb of the Hindoos: "Yes indeed, he was the first man; no wonder that he is wise."

President Charles Cuthbert Hall founds his book "Does God Send Trouble?" on this verse eleven of the fifteenth chapter. The consolations Eliphaz refers to are those the three friends had been giving Job, thinking them derived from God.

"From their fathers" (xv. 18). "The gray-headed and the very aged men, much elder than thy father." He now presents a string of maxims and oracles from the fathers. These maxims are true, but evidently Eliphaz applies them to Job.

"A stiff neck" (xv. 26), "like a bull, which rushes blindly against whatever arouses its wrath."

"Bosses" (xv. 26) are the knobs on the convex part of the shield, facing the foe. "Buckler," a shield fastened with a buckle.

[1] Job xv. 2, 3, 6–9, 11, 14–18, 20, 21, 24–26, 33.

The vine when it fruits is very open to various forms of disease in which its unripened grapes fall like leaves in the autumn.

The Syrian olive bears very copiously every other year. But even in the years when it rests from bearing it blossoms, the blossoms falling off before the berry is formed. "In the spring one may see the bloom, on the slightest breath of wind shed like snowflakes and perishing by millions." (From Cox, "Commentary on Job," p. 197.)

JOB (chapters xvi, xvii).

> I have heard many such things:
> Miserable comforters are ye all.
> I also could speak as ye do;
> If your soul were in my soul's stead,
> I could join words together against you,
> And shake mine head at you.
> But I would strengthen you with my mouth,
> And the solace of my lips should assuage your grief.

> Mine adversary sharpeneth his eyes upon me.
> They have gaped upon me with their mouth;
> They have smitten me upon the cheek reproachfully:
> They gather themselves together against me.
> God delivereth me to the ungodly,
> Although there is no violence in mine hands,
> And my prayer is pure.

> O earth, cover not thou my blood,
> And let my cry have no resting place.
> Even now, behold, my Witness is in heaven,
> And He that voucheth for me is on high.
> My friends scorn me:
> But mine eye poureth out tears unto God;
> That he would maintain the right of a man with God,
> And of a son of man with his neighbor.[1]

[1] The margin reads for these last two lines:
> "That one might plead for a man with God,
> As a son of man pleadeth for his neighbor."

But return ye, all of you, and come now!
And I shall not find a wise man among you.

If I look for Sheol as mine house;
If I have spread my couch in the darkness;
If I have said to corruption, Thou art my father;
To the worm, Thou art my mother, and my sister;
Where then is my hope? [1]

"Miserable comforters" (xvi. 2) in reply to Eliphaz's question (xv. 1), "Are the consolations of God too small for thee?" The friends were giving just the reverse of consolation.

Job is beginning, in xvi. 10, to distinguish between the God pictured by his friends who afflicts him because He hates him, and the true God who loves him while He afflicts him.

The best commentary on this outburst of resentment at the Friends' consolations is found in a passage from "Much Ado About Nothing" (Act v, Sc. 1), in which Shakespeare may have had this plaint of Job in mind. Leonato, maddened with grief, says:

"I pray thee cease thy counsel
Which falls into mine ear as profitless
As water in a sieve: give me not counsel;
Nor let no comforter delight mine ear
But such an one whose wrongs do suit with mine.
Bring me a father that so loved his child,
Whose joy of her is overwhelm'd like mine,
And bid him speak of patience.
If such an one will smile and stroke his beard,
Patch grief with proverb; bring him yet to me
And I of him will gather patience."

"And my prayer is pure," (xvi. 17). "A profound yet very practical test of one's integrity before God. One is reminded of Coleridge's 'Ancient Mariner,' who relates that as soon as he could look on God's creatures with love instead of hatred, 'that self-same moment I could pray.'"

Compare Job xvi. 18 with the challenge of Queen Constance:

"Arm, arm, you heavens, against these perjured kings!" (Shakespeare, "King John," Act iii, Sc. 1.)

"Witness" (xvi. 19), Advocate, the Daysman of ix. 33.

[1] Job xvi. 2, 4, 5, 9, 10, 17–21; xvii. 10, 13–15.

BILDAD (chapter xviii).

> How long will ye lay snares for words?
> Consider, and afterwards we will speak.
> Wherefore are we counted as beasts,
> And are become unclean in your sight?

> Thou that tearest thyself in thine anger,
> Shall the earth be forsaken for thee?
> Or shall the rock be removed out of its place?

> Yea, the light of the wicked shall be put out,
> And the spark of his fire shall not shine.
> And his own counsel shall cast him down.

> For he is cast into a net by his own feet,
> And he walketh upon the toils.
> And calamity shall be ready for his halting.
> And he shall be brought to the king of terrors.
> And chased out of the world.
> Such are the dwellings of the unrighteous,
> And this is the place of him that knoweth not God.[1]

All of Bildad's proverbial sayings are allusions to Job's character and sufferings, and he evidently intended that Job should see his own portrait in the picture.

"Web . . . toils." In verses 8–10 the poet brings together all, or nearly all, the Hebrew names for the various kinds of nets and traps. We see the sinner who once strode along "the primrose path," now creeping along through dark and pathless shades strewn with traps and snares, starting at the fall of every leaf, peopling the darkness with spectres, often pausing to listen, in the vain hope of escaping the visible and invisible perils to which he is exposed.

> "When all that is within him doth condemn
> Itself for being there."
> (Cox, "Commentary on Job," p. 225.)

[1] Job xviii. 2–5, 7, 8, 12, 14, 18, 21.

JOB (chapter xix).

> How long will ye vex my soul,
>   And break me in pieces with words?
> These ten times have ye reproached me:
>   Ye are not ashamed that ye deal hardly with me.

> Behold I cry out of wrong but I am not heard.
> He hath stripped me of my glory,
>   And taken the crown from my head.
> He hath broken me down on every side, and I am gone:
>   And mine hope hath he plucked up like a tree.

> He hath put my brethren far from me,
>   And mine acquaintance are wholly estranged from me.
> My kinsfolk have failed,
>   And my familiar friends have forgotten me.
> They that dwell in mine house, and my maids,
>   Count me for a stranger.
> Even young children despise me;
>   If I arise, they speak against me.
> All my inward friends abhor me:
>   And they whom I loved are turned against me.
> My bone cleaveth to my skin and to my flesh,
>   And I am escaped with the skin of my teeth.

> Have pity upon me, have pity upon me,
>   O ye my friends,
> For the hand of God hath touched me!

> Oh that my words were now written!
> Oh that they were inscribed in a book!
> That with an iron pen and lead
> They were graven in the rock for ever!

𝔍𝔫𝔰𝔠𝔯𝔦𝔭𝔱𝔦𝔬𝔫 𝔬𝔫 𝔱𝔥𝔢 𝔯𝔬𝔠𝔨.

For I know that my Redeemer liveth,
And that He shall stand up at the last upon the earth;
And after my skin hath been thus destroyed,
Yet from my flesh shall I see God!

Whom I shall see for myself,[1]
And mine eyes shall behold and not another.

> —My reins are consumed within me—
> > (*He nearly faints. A pause.*)
> If ye say, How we will persecute him!
> Be ye afraid of the sword:
> That ye may know there is a judgment.[2]

Job acknowledges his sufferings, how could he help it? His words should have touched them with pity. But he denies Bildad's accusation that it was his own conduct that brought these things upon him. It was God that had sent his affliction; and his friends and neighbors made it harder to bear. But God would vindicate him from all the false aspersions cast upon him, would deliver him from his afflictions.

"Oh, that my words" (xix. 23), referring to the six lines beginning with "I know that my Redeemer liveth," which Job desired to have inscribed in book and on rock to endure as long as the memory of the sufferer survived among men, as his dying testimony to the goodness and justice of God.

"Iron and lead." (xix. 24.) The iron engraved the words on the rock, and molten lead was poured into the lines thus made to make them both more legible and permanent. The statement of Job's faith in a Redeemer, says Chrysostom, has been written far more durably than on rock with pen of iron. "They are graven on the Rock of God's Word, and there they are still read, and minister comfort to all generations."

"I know that my Redeemer liveth." These six lines (xix. 25–27) have attracted more attention and have been more variously interpreted than any other passage in the book. For these opinions see the commentators. Here there is only room for a brief statement of what seems to be the true interpretation.

---

[1] Margin, "on my side.
[2] Job xix. 2, 3, 7, 9, 10, 13–15, 18–21, 23–29.

"My Redeemer," Hebrew, my "Goel." The word denotes the next of kin, whose duty it was to avenge the blood of a murdered man (see Num. xxxv. 19), and to succor the bereaved and needy (see Ruth iii. 9-13; iv. 1-8). (Genung, "Epic of the Inner Life," p. 236.)

"The term *redeemer* (Heb. *goel*) is frequently used of God as the deliverer of his people out of captivity, e. g., very often in Is. xl, *seq.* (xlix. 7, 26; liv. 5, 8), and also as the deliverer of individuals from distress (Gen. xlviii. 16; Ps. xix. 14; ciii. 4). . . . Thus the ideas of Goel and Redeemer virtually coincide." (Davidson, "Cambridge Bible," p. 143.)

He had longed for a Daysman; he hoped for an Advocate; now he knows that his Redeemer, the Vindicator of his innocence, the Deliverer from his troubles, is the Living God.

"He shall stand" (xix. 25), arise, appear, come forward as a witness, do a kinsman's part for me.

"Upon the earth;" most prefer "over my dust." "Over my grave" he will appear for me, clad in robes of victory and justice.

"And after my skin" (xix. 26), probably his body, for Job had just complained (ver. 20) that nothing was left of him but skin and bone; after the last fibre of his body had been consumed.

"Hath been thus destroyed" (probably pointing to his emaciated frame). The verb implies extreme violence, as if his disease were a wild beast rending and ravaging his body. The meaning is "when I have died under the ravages of my disease."

"Yet from my flesh." The Hebrew preposition is variously translated "from," "in," "out of," "without." "From" is the literal translation and may mean (1) in my flesh—Job in his body, looking out from his body, sees God. Or (2) it may mean free from, stripped from his body, he as a spirit will see God.

There are some curious examples of this double sense of " from " in Shakespeare, as in "Richard III," Act iv, Sc. 4, in the dialogue between King Richard and Queen Elizabeth; and in "King Lear," Act ii, Sc. 1, Regan says, "To answer *from* our home."

"Whom I shall see for myself" (xix. 27), and not through the report of another. Death does not end all with him. He will be alive beyond death and enjoy his vindication. "The early Hebrews had no manner of doubt, any more than we have, that the soul or spiritual part of man survived the body." (Prof. James Orr of Glasgow.) [1]

This passage is one of those outbursts of hope, those glimpses of victory in the great battle which Job was waging, which are like the songs of triumph—the song of Moses and the Lamb, and the glimpses of final redemption, which emerge now and then in the great conflict of the Kingdom of Heaven in Revela-

[1] See Prof. Max Müller's "Anthropological Religion, or Belief in Immortality in the Old Testament," pp. 367, 377.

tion, between the appearance of Christ in chapter i, and the New Jerusalem in chapters xxi, xxii. As there, so with Job, the darkness and conflict returned, but never so hopeless as before. His experience here was like a brief glimpse of sunshine through the rifted clouds. The storm burst again upon him, but there was a brighter hope of the clearing skies. Maspero's translation of inscriptions on the pyramids shows that the Eygptians, centuries before Moses, believed in the resurrection.[1]

ZOPHAR (chapter xx). (*Interrupting.*)
I have heard the reproof which putteth me to shame.
　　Knowest thou not this of old time,
　　Since man was placed upon earth,
That the triumphing of the wicked is short,
And the joy of the godless but for a moment?
　　Though his excellency mount up to the heavens,
　　And his head reach unto the clouds;
Yet he shall perish for ever like his own dung:
They which have seen him shall say, Where is he?
He shall fly away as a dream, and shall not be found:
Yea, he shall be chased away as a vision of the night.

God shall cast the fierceness of his wrath upon him,
And shall it rain upon him while he is eating.
The Heavens shall reveal his iniquity,
And the earth shall rise up against him.

　　This is the portion of a wicked man from God,
　　And the heritage appointed unto him by God.[2]

　　Job had rejected Zophar's counsel and refuted his teachings, and threatened him with judgment—him the pink and pattern of a good man. It was intolerable. He therefore returns to his charge, that the triumphing of the wicked was short, even as Job's had been. He declares that the "terrible and ignominious end of all his (Job's) greatness was simply the natural and inevitable outcome of his heinous and notorious crimes." He had worn "a golden sorrow," but it was a crown of thorns.

[1] See Orr's "Christian View of God and the World," Appendix to Lecture V, on the "Old Testament Doctrine of Immortality."
[2] Job xx. 3–8, 23, 27, 29.

JOB (chapter xxi).

Hear diligently my speech,
And let this be your consolations.
Suffer me, and I also will speak:
And after that I have spoken, mock on.

As for me, is my complaint to man?
And why should I not be impatient?

Mark me, and be astonished,
And lay your hand upon your mouth.
Even when I remember I am troubled,
And horror taketh hold on my flesh.

Wherefore do the wicked live,
Become old, yea, wax mighty in power?
Their seed is established with them in their sight,
And their offspring before their eyes.
Their houses are safe from fear,
Neither is the rod of God upon them.
Yet they said unto God, "Depart from us,
For we desire not the knowledge of thy ways.
What is the Almighty that we should serve him?
And what profit should we have if we pray unto him?"

(*Eliphaz* ?)
Lo, their prosperity is not in their hand:
The counsel of the wicked is far from me.[1]

(*Job*)
How oft is it that the lamp of the wicked is put out?
That they are as stubble before the wind,
And as chaff that the storm carrieth away?

(*Zophar* ?)
Shall any teach God knowledge.[1]

[1] Professor Moulton puts these three lines in the mouths of Eliphaz and Zophar, who interrupt Job. Others regard them as objections or questions spoken by Job as interpreting the thoughts of the friends, and then answered by Job.

(Job)

One dieth in his full strength,
Being wholly at ease and quiet:
His breasts are full of milk,
And the marrow of his bones is moistened.
And another dieth in bitterness of soul,
And never tasteth of good.
They lie down alike in the dust,
And the worm covereth them.

(*The* FRIENDS *offer to interrupt.*)

Behold, I know your thoughts,
And the devices which ye wrongfully imagine against me.[1]

"Your consolations," (xxi. 2). "The consolations of God" of which
Eliphaz had spoken (xv. 11).

Job controverts the position of Zophar by showing that his principle does
not work in actual life. The wicked are not always treated in this world according to their wickedness. Therefore the good also are not always treated as one
would expect the good to be treated. You cannot tell by his prosperity whether
a man is good or not.

"Be astonished" (xxi. 5) as Job himself was at the mystery of his sufferings,
and of the prosperity of the wicked.

THE RESULTANT OF THE SECOND COLLOQUY

The Second Colloquy marks a decided and a large advance in the action
of the drama. The Friends advance by narrowing their position to necessary
and vital points. They also advance by changing "the urbane tones of invitation" in the first Colloquy to the "shrill accents of invective and denunciation."
They express their feelings more openly. And invective itself is a sign of the
weakness of their argument.

Job advances to a more reasonable and hopeful tone. The "consolations"
of his friends do not irritate him so much. But most of all he gains in faith and
in the assurance of the righteousness of God. He sees his Redeemer and
Vindicator in the next world. Sheol is no longer a land of gloom, with shadowy
joys, and shadowy griefs, but a real, full life, morally connected with the present
life, in which the justice denied men here would run its full course.

Such is the immense spoil which Job now carries off from his conflict with
Death and Despair. Out of the very ruins created by Despair he has built up
the Great Hope of a retributive life beyond the grave. (Condensed from
Prof. Samuel Cox, "Commentary on Job," pp. 287-90.)

[1] Job xxi. 2-9, 14-18.

THE THIRD CYCLE OF SPEECHES

ELIPHAZ (chapter xxii).

Can a man be profitable unto God?
Is it any pleasure to the Almighty that thou art righteous?
Is not thy wickedness great?
Neither is there any end to thine iniquities.
For thou hast taken pledges of thy brother for nought,
And stripped the naked of their clothing.
Thou hast not given water to the weary to drink,
And thou hast withholden bread from the hungry.
Thou hast sent widows away empty,
And the arms of the fatherless have been broken.
Therefore snares are round about thee,
And sudden fear troubleth thee.

Is not God in the height of heaven?
And behold the height of the stars, how high they are!
And thou sayest, "What doth God know?
Can he judge through the thick darkness?
Thick clouds are a covering to him, that he seeth not;
And he walketh in the circuit of heaven."

Wilt thou keep the old way
Which wicked men have trodden?
Who said unto God, Depart from us;
And, What can the Almighty do for us?
Yet he filled their houses with good things.

Acquaint now thyself with him and be at peace:
Thereby good shall come unto thee.
Receive, I pray thee, the law from his mouth,
And lay up his words in thine heart.

If thou return to the Almighty, thou shalt be built up;
If thou put away unrighteousness far from thy tents.
And the Almighty shall be thy treasure.
And light shall shine upon thy ways.[1]

"Is it any pleasure," (xxii. 3.) They had not heard of the joy of the angels over one sinner that repenteth. The argument of Eliphaz is that "God is punishing Job. It cannot be for righteousness. Hence it must be for wickedness." (Genung, "Epic of the Inner Life," p. 252.)

"Is not thy wickedness great?" Eliphaz breaks out in verses 5–10 in a string of charges of which he has no proof. He pictures Job not as he is, but as he ought to be according to the dogma the Friends hold, that sin is the sole cause of suffering.

It is interesting to notice that the last words of Eliphaz unconsciously predicted the final issue of this great drama.

JOB (chapters xxiii, xxiv).
Oh that I knew where I might find him,
That I might come even to his seat!
I would order my cause before him,
And fill my mouth with arguments.
I would know the words which he would answer me,
And understand what he would say unto me.
Would he contend with me in the greatness of his power?
Nay, but he would give heed unto me:

Behold I go forward, but he is not there;
And backward, but I cannot perceive him:
On the left hand, when he doth work, but I cannot behold him.
He hideth himself on the right hand, that I cannot see him.

But he knoweth the way that I take;
When he hath tried me, I shall come forth as gold.[2]

[1] Job xxii. 2, 3, 5–7, 9, 10, 12–15, 17, 18, 21–23, 25, 28.
[2] Job xxiii. 3–6, 8–10.

BILDAD (chapter xxv).

> Dominion and fear are with him;
> He maketh peace in his high places.
> Is there any number of his armies?
> And upon whom doth not his light arise?
> How then can man be just before God?
> Or how can he be clean that is born of a woman?
> Behold, even the moon hath no brightness,
> And the stars are not pure in his sight:
> How much less man, that is a worm!
> And the son of man, which is a worm! [1]

It will be noticed that this is the last speech of the three Friends; some think that this is an imperfection, and that the following chapters are an addition to the original book. Professor Moulton thinks that the speeches here have become intermingled. He gives Bildad more than is assigned to him in our Bibles, taken from Job's speeches, and from those speeches he also assigns a portion to Zophar, thus making the third cycle complete like the others.

But the book is more poetic as it is. The Friends have said all there was for them to say and their argument is incomplete like the cycle of their speeches. And the sayings which do not seem to express Job's sentiments may be, as many think, quotations by Job of statements he wishes to answer.

JOB (chapter xxvi).

> He stretcheth out the north over empty space,
> And hangeth the earth upon nothing.
> He bindeth up the waters in his thick clouds;
>> The pillars of heaven tremble
>> And are astonished at his rebuke.
> He stirreth up the sea with his power.
>
> Lo, these are but the outskirts of his ways;
> And how small a whisper do we hear of him!
> But the thunder of his power who can understand? [2]

[1] Job xxv. 2–6.
[2] Job xxvi. 7, 8 11, 12, 14.

The Debate ends here. Then follow two Soliloquies of JOB, *and his "Oath of Clearing," chapters xxvii–xxxi, each beginning with "And* JOB *again took up his parable and said." He speaks to the mixed audience, the* THREE FRIENDS, ELIHU, *relatives, neighbors, and citizens.*

FIRST SOLILOQUY. (Chapters xxvii, xxviii.)

Job first summons God as his witness—"As God liveth." Then he passes on to a general summing up of the facts about the wicked and their suffering.

"The connection of the 28th chapter with the rest of the book has been a puzzle to some. But does it not follow naturally? Having portrayed the extreme of unwisdom (with which in the old philosophy wickedness was identified), the life that has not the future nor is built therefor, it is natural that Job should next speak of its contrast, the true wisdom and foresight whereby to build human life and character. There are many marvelous things that man may know or search out; but many also are unsearchable. He cannot see as God sees, perhaps cannot reach absolute truth. But there is a wisdom *for him*, which points to the absolute good as the needle points to the pole." (Genung, "Epic of the Inner Life," p. 277.)

JOB (*in monologue*).

Surely there is a mine for silver,
And a place for gold which they refine.
Iron is taken out of the earth,
And brass is molten out of the stone.
As for the earth, out of it cometh bread.
The stones thereof are the place of sapphires,
And it hath dust of gold.
But where shall wisdom be found?
And where is the place of understanding?
Man knoweth not the price thereof;
Neither is it found in the land of the living.
The deep saith, It is not in me:
And the sea saith, It is not with me.
It cannot be gotten for gold,
Neither shall silver be weighed for the price thereof.
It cannot be valued with the gold of Ophir,
With the precious onyx, or the sapphire.
Yea, the price of wisdom is above rubies.

The topaz of Ethiopia shall not equal it,
   Neither shall it be valued with pure gold.
Whence then cometh wisdom?
And where is the place of understanding?
Destruction and Death say,
   We have heard a rumor thereof with our ears.
GOD understandeth the way thereof,
And he knoweth the place thereof.

He established it, yea, and searched it out.
   And unto man he said,
      Behold, the fear of the Lord, that is wisdom ;
      And to depart from evil is understanding.[1]

Compare the praise of Wisdom in the early chapters of Proverbs.

SECOND SOLILOQUY. JOB'S REVIEW OF HIS LIFE. (Chapters xxix, xxx.)

"Having thus reached the culmination of his argument, Job here, in a retrospect, gathers up the threads of his past life and his present affliction, to present them as his vindication before God." (Genung, p. 283.)

The description of his trial from his loathsome disease, with which the monologue closes, ends with a verse of idylic beauty and sweetness (Job xxx. 31):

Therefore is my harp turned to mourning,
   And my pipe unto the voice of them that weep.

The harp and pipe (flute) were instruments of mirth. The festive music of his life has been broken into harsh discords. (See Cox, "Commentary on Job," p. 389.)

THE OATH OF CLEARING. (Chapter xxxi.)

JOB (*rising and lifting his hands*).

If I have walked with vanity,
And my foot hath hasted to deceit;
   (Let me be weighed in an even balance,
   That God may know my integrity;)

[1] Job xxviii. 1, 2, 5, 6, 12-16, 18-20, 22, 23, 27, 28.

If my step hath turned out of the way,
And mine heart walked after mine eyes
And if any spot hath cleaved to mine hands:
THEN LET ME SOW, AND LET ANOTHER EAT;
YEA, LET THE PRODUCE OF MY FIELD BE ROOTED OUT.

If I have withheld the poor from their desire,
Or have caused the eyes of the widow to fail;
Or have eaten my morsel alone,
And the fatherless hath not eaten thereof;
If I have seen any perish for want of clothing,
And if he were not warmed with the fleece of my sheep;
If I have lifted up my hand against the fatherless,
Because I saw my help in the gate:
THEN LET MY SHOULDER FALL FROM THE SHOULDER BLADE,
AND MINE ARM BE BROKEN FROM THE BONE.

If I have made gold my hope,
And have said to the fine gold, Thou art my confidence;
If I rejoice because my wealth was great,
And because mine hand had gotten much;
THIS ALSO WERE AN INIQUITY TO BE PUNISHED BY THE JUDGES:
FOR I SHOULD HAVE LIED TO GOD THAT IS ABOVE.

If I rejoiced at the destruction of him that hated me,
Or lifted up myself when evil found him.
If like Adam I covered my transgressions,
By hiding mine iniquity in my bosom;
Because I feared the great multitude.
If my land cry out against me,
And the furrows thereof weep together;
If I have eaten the fruits thereof without money,
Or have caused the owners thereof to lose their life:
LET THISTLES GROW INSTEAD OF WHEAT,
AND COCKLE INSTEAD OF BARLEY!

Oh that I had one to hear me!
(Lo, here is my signature, let the Almighty answer me.)
   The words of Job are ended![1]

"Here is my signature," (xxxi. 35). Here is my sign, my mark. "Many an Arab chieftain could do no more at this day than affix his mark; and a hundred years ago it may be doubted whether more than one English squire in ten could have done more." (Cox, "Commentary on Job," p. 400.)

THE OUTCOME OF THE DISCUSSION

1. Job had come to believe that

God is good and just in spite of evil in the world;

although he could not see how that truth could be reconciled with the fact of his sufferings. He had rebelled not against the true God, but against the false picture of God the three Friends had presented, "a true Medusa's head, the very look at which turned him to stone."

Job was victorious over his own doubts and fears.

Compare the "Everlasting No" of Carlyle's "Sartor Resartus," Bk. ii, chap. 7.

"To me the Universe was all void of Life, of Purpose, of Volition, even of Hostility. It was one huge dead, immeasurable Steam-engine, rolling on in its dead indifference to grind me limb from limb. . . . All at once there arose a Thought in me, and I asked myself, What art thou afraid of? Death? Hast thou not a heart, canst thou not suffer whatso it be; and as a child of Freedom, though outcast, trample Tophet itself under thy feet? Let it come then. I will meet it and defy it. . . . Thus had the EVERLASTING No pealed authoritatively through all the recesses of my Being, of my ME; and then was it that my whole ME stood up, in native God-created majesty, and with emphasis recorded its Protest. Such a Protest, the most important transaction in Life, may that same Indignation and Defiance, in a psychological point of view, be fitly called. The Everlasting No had said: 'Behold, thou art fatherless, outcast, and the Universe is mine' (the Devil's); to which my whole Me now made answer: '*I* am not thine, but Free, and forever hate thee!' . . . It is from this hour that I date my spiritual new birth. . . . Perhaps I directly thereupon began to be a MAN."

Compare and contrast Æschylus's "Prometheus Bound," who is "the Job of the heathen." He, one of the gods, hoped to confer great blessings on men by giving to them the knowledge of fire which he stole from heaven, and carried

[1] Job xxxi. 5-8, 16, 17, 19-22, 24, 25, 28, 29, 33, 34, 38-40, 35, 40.

to earth "concealed in a stalk of fennel, that men might learn to forge tools and instruments, and so arts and wealth might arise upon the earth." Jupiter was angry at this, for he had little care for human happiness and designed to sweep away the human race. "Prometheus therefore rescued man not merely from a brute life, but from death itself." It was for this good act that Prometheus was chained to the peak of the Caucasus mountains, there to linger out the long years of eternity, while an eagle is sent to feed constantly on his living flesh. But Prometheus defies the lightnings of the supreme deity, Jupiter. He will not yield, for he is right, and has done right; and Jupiter is unjust and unkind, and shows it by bringing a great storm and earthquake; "the earth opens, and Prometheus with the rock to which he is chained sinks into the abyss." "In the Greek play Prometheus represents the cause of man against Jupiter, and openly rebels against him. . . . Now, so long as the supreme God is represented as wicked or unjust, such an attitude can be an object of sympathy ('we love him, and admire his courage and high spirit'); but to those who believe in the true God, a rebel against him cannot be regarded as a friend to man, or be an object of anything but hatred." Hence Job's friends were so earnest to prove that Job had done wrong instead of God. "In Prometheus the sovereignty of the supreme God becomes assured only when Wisdom and Power shall have entered into indissoluble union." Job comes to trust in the eternal goodness and justice of God, that somehow

> "good shall fall
> At last—far off—at last, to all";

although he knew that he was but

> "An infant crying in the night:
> An infant crying for the light:
> And with no language but a cry."
> (Tennyson, "In Memoriam," liv.)

Trusting God in the dark shows more faith, cultivates faith more, than to merely know half the truths in the universe. Knowledge is good, but Trust and Love are better.

2. Job held also to the fact that he was innocent of any conduct which could justly result in his suffering so much more than other men. He did not know, as we know, that his sufferings were sent because he was good, as in the case of martyrs and reformers. By his faith in God in spite of these sufferings, while he felt that he did not deserve them, he shows that he stood Satan's test. He was right in denying the accusations of his friends. For if they had been true he would have failed in the test.

Compare the "Everlasting Yea" of Carlyle.

"Foreshadows, call them rather foresplendors, of that Truth and Beginning of Truths, fell mysteriously over my soul. Sweeter than Dayspring to the

Shipwrecked in Nova Zembla; ah! like the mother's voice to her little child that strays bewildered . . . came that Evangel—The Universe is not dead and demoniacal, a charnel house with spectres, but Godlike and my Father's. There is in man a Higher than Love of Happiness: he can do without Happiness, and instead thereof find Blessedness. Was it not to preach forth this same Higher that sages and martyrs, the Poet and the Priest, in all times, have spoken and suffered, bearing testimony, through life and through death, of the Godlike that is in Man, and how in the Godlike only has he Strength and Freedom? . . . Love not Pleasure; love God. This is the Everlasting Yea, wherein all contradiction is solved; wherein whoso walks and works it is well with him." ("Sartor Resartus," Bk. ii, chap. 9.)

THE SECOND SOLUTION OF THE PROBLEM OF SUFFERING

That sometimes suffering is the fruit and punishment of sin; but no one knows enough to judge his fellow man, and decide from the suffering how much, if any, is due to his guilt.

THE TENDENCY AMONG MEN IS TO JUDGE OTHERS. So in John ix. the disciples ask, "Who did sin, this man or his parents, that he should be born blind?" So in Luke xiii. 1–5, concerning those on whom the tower of Siloam fell. A good man's son goes astray, and you immediately hear that his father's training was not good. A man fails in business, and men look for some weakness or bad judgment. No one knows enough to judge others correctly. Compare the three Johns in each John, and the three Thomases in each Thomas, as shown by Dr. Holmes in his "Autocrat of the Breakfast-Table," chapter iii. (1) the real John; known only to his Maker. (2) John's ideal John, never the real one, and often very unlike him. (3) Thomas's ideal John, never the real John, nor John's John, but often very unlike either. And a similar division for Thomas, of (1) the real Thomas, (2) Thomas's ideal Thomas, and (3) John's ideal Thomas.

See the hymn "Think gently of the erring one," especially the lines

> "Heir of the same inheritance,
>   Child of the self-same God,
> He hath but stumbled in the path
>   We have in weakness trod."
>   (Miss Fletcher.)

A friend once said to the Bishop of London: "How is it that you always think of something pleasant to say about everybody under the sun?" The bishop laughed. "Well, you see," he replied, "there is so much good in the worst of us and so much bad in the best of us that it does not become any of us to speak ill of the rest of us."

THE TENDENCY OF SOME TO MISJUDGE THEMSELVES. There are certain sensitive souls who when some misfortune comes upon them feel sure that it is on account of some special sin. More in former days than now a mother who had lost her child felt that it was taken away because she loved it too much, made an idol of it. See some fine remarks on this in Miss Havergal's "Kept for the Master's Use."

> *Eleanor.* "I tremble when I think how much I love him."
> *Beatrice.* "Do you love him as much as Christ loves us?
> . . . .
> Then till you reach the standard of that love
> Let neither fears nor well-meant warning voice
> Distress you with 'too much.'"
> *Eleanor.* "But 'tis written, 'Keep yourselves from idols.'
> How shall I obey?"
> *Beatrice.* "Oh, not by loving less, but loving more.
> It is not that we love our precious ones
> Too much, but God too little."

SUFFERING IS SOMETIMES THE FRUIT AND PUNISHMENT OF SIN. The natural outcome of sin is suffering. The natural fruit of wrong-doing is pain and woe. This is true as a general principle and tendency. It is true of nations and of communities. A virtuous and temperate community will be more prosperous in every way than a vicious, drunken, idle, dishonest community. Take young men as a class, and those who keep free from vices and intemperance, who are diligent, honest, and religious, stand the best chance for worldly success. And this is the promise of God, both in the Old Testament and the New. It is the fruit also of God's laws in nature. And this is necessary in order to prove that God is on the side of goodness. If hell were the fruit of virtue, and heaven the reward of vice, it would be impossible to prove that God is good.

> "Howe'er we trust to mortal things,
> Each hath its pair of folded wings;
> Though long their terrors rest unspread,
> Their fatal plumes are never shed;
> At last, at last, they stretch in flight,
> And blot the day and blast the night!"
> (O. W. Holmes, "After the Fire.")

The Bible, both in the Old Testament and in the New Testament, declares over and over again that punishment must and will follow sin. "Every sin contains within itself the seed of its own punishment—but not every seed matures" in the moral world any more than in the physical world.

"Natural laws are God's work, right and kind, the best for man in his present state of being." They cannot be improved. "Sin is wrong adjustment to right laws. . . . And this accounts for all the physical and material sorrow, sickness, misery, poverty, bitterness, violence, death in the world." (Charles Cuthbert Hall, D.D., "Does God Send Trouble?")

And this is necessary in order to save the world from sin. Punishments are small evils compared with sin.

"The work of the Avenger is a necessity. It is part of God's philanthropy. There are hells on earth into which no breath of Heaven can ever come; these must be swept away. There are social soils in which only unrighteousness can flourish; these must be broken up.

"And that is the work of the Day of Vengeance. When is that day? It is now. Who is the Avenger? Law. What Law? Criminal Law, Sanitary Law, Social Law, Natural Law. Wherever the poor are trodden upon or tread upon one another; wherever the air is poison and the water foul; wherever want stares, and vice reigns, and rags rot—there the Avenger takes his stand. . . . Delay him not. He is the messenger of Christ. Despair of him not, distrust him not. His Day dawns slowly, but his work is sure. Though evil stalks the world, it is on the way to execution; though wrong reigns, it must end in self-combustion. The very nature of things is God's Avenger; the very story of civilization is the history of Christ's Throne." (Prof. Henry Drummond in "The Programme of Christianity.")

THE OLD TESTAMENT abounds in statement and historic illustrations of the fact that disobedience to God is followed by punishment. The ravages of heathen nations which overwhelmed the Jews; the disasters which came from Nature—the plagues of Egypt, the locusts, the drought, the blight, the famine—are all punishments of the people's sins. So in the terrible chapters of promises and warning in Deuteronomy (chapters xxviii–xxx) which aroused Josiah to reform his people. The prophets are full of these statements till we almost weary of their warnings.

THE NEW TESTAMENT inculcates the same warnings, but with larger hope of forgiveness, with a fuller revelation of love, with a clearer revelation of the desire of God to save, and of the way of salvation, but with never a lessening of the fact that punishment follows sin, and the only way to escape its consequences is to turn from the sin itself.

Even the warning of Jesus against judging others in his teaching about those on whom the tower of Siloam fell, does not change his attitude toward sin, for he adds, "but except ye repent ye shall all likewise perish" (Luke xiii. 3), and they did at the destruction of Jerusalem, forty years later. And he said to the man healed at the pool of Bethesda, "Sin no more, lest a worse thing befall thee." (John v. 14.) "There are more than forty statements to this effect in the New Testament."

It is the law of the harvest that we reap what we sow. "Be not deceived, God is not mocked; for whatsoever a man soweth, that shall he also reap." (Gal. vi. 7.)

"The tissue of the life to be,
We weave with colors all our own,
And in the field of destiny
We reap as we have sown."
(See Peloubet, "Loom of Life," p. 40.)

"Sow an act and reap a habit, sow a habit and reap a character, sow a character and reap a destiny."

"I saw far down the coming time
The fiery chastisement of crime,
With noise of mingling hosts, and jar
Of falling towers and shouts of war,
I saw the nations rise and fall,
Like fire-gleams on my tent's white wall."
(Whittier, "Ezekiel.")

LA CONSCIENCE.—"Every one knows Victor Hugo's beautiful poem, 'La Conscience,' the story of Cain fleeing away before the Eye of God. He walks thirty days and thirty nights, until he reaches the shores of the ocean. 'Let us stop here,' says he. But as he sits down his face turns pale; he has seen ' in the mournful skies the Eye at the same place.' His sons, full of awe, try to erect barriers between him and the Eye: a tent, then a wall of iron, then a tower, and a city; but all is vain. 'I see the Eye still,' cries the unhappy man. At last they dig a tomb; the father is put into it. But
'Though overhead they closed the awful vault,
The Eye was in the tomb, and looked on Cain.'"
(Rev. Reuben Saillens, D.D.)

At a meeting of the Medical Society in Boston, President Eliot told the doctors that while the belief in a future hell was not so great as it once was, it was their business to warn young men that if they indulged in certain sins they would find a hell on earth.

One of the most effective books on this subject is "Plutarch on the Delay of Divine Justice."[1] It is full of illustrations. He says (p. 24), "It may be well for us to listen to Hesiod, who maintains, not with Plato, that punishment is a suffering that follows wrong-doing, but that it is a twin birth with wrong-doing, springing from the same soil and the same root." "Guilt in the very act of wrong-doing receives its penalty." "Some persons are like children, who often, seeing in the theatres malefactors in gold-embroidered tunics and purple mantles, crowned and dancing, admire and applaud them as happy beings, until they appear on the stage goaded, and scourged, and with fire streaming from their gay and finely wrought apparel."

ALL LITERATURE AND ALL HISTORY are full of examples of this great warning fact. Byron laments:

[1] Translated and edited by Prof. A. P. Peabody of Harvard. (Little, Brown & Co., $1.00.)

" No ear can hear, nor tongue can tell
   The tortures of that inward hell."
                    ("The Giaour," l. 748.)

The ghosts of those slain by Richard III haunted him with their horrors
till he exclaims:

"My conscience hath a thousand several tongues
   And every tongue brings in a several tale,
   And every tale condemns me for a villain."
            (Shakespeare, "King Richard III," Act v, Sc. 3.)

One by one they appear in the vision before him, just before his last battle,
rehearse the crimes he had committed upon them, and cry, "Despair and die.
Let me sit heavy on thy soul to-morrow."

"Every man's conscience is a thousand men." ("Richard III," Act v,
Sc. 2.)

Lady Macbeth, walking in her sleep, exclaims: "All the perfumes of Arabia
cannot sweeten this little hand." ("Macbeth," Act v, Sc. 1.)

Nero was haunted by the ghost of his mother whom he had put to death.
Caligula suffered from want of sleep, being haunted by the faces of his murdered
victims. The Furies of classic mythology "are commonly represented as bran-
dishing each a torch in one hand and a scourge of snakes in the other."

"I know no poem since Macbeth that so portrays the agony of an awakened
conscience as Browning's 'Pippa Passes.'" (President Stanley Hall, "A
Study of Fears.") See also Hawthorne's "Mosses from an Old Manse," vol. ii,
The Bosom Serpent, where the chief character continually exclaims, "It gnaws
me"; Hood's Poems, "Eugene Aram"; the Legend of the Troll in the preface
to Hall Caine's "The Bondman." N. P. Willis, Poems, "Parrhasius";

"Ambition only, gives
   Even of bitterness, a beaker full."

"I sat alone with my conscience
   In a place where time had ceased,
And we talked of my former living
   In the land where the years increased.
The ghosts of forgotten actions
   Came floating before my sight,
And things that I thought were dead things,
   Were alive with a terrible might;
The vision of all my past life
   Was an awful thing to face,
Alone with my conscience sitting
   In that silently solemn place."
            (Anon. in "Uplands of God," p. 62.)

See Joseph Cook's "Monday Lectures: Conscience," which is effective. "Of terrible power is the description of Judas, who, like 'staring Orestes, with eyes flung back upon his mother's ghost,' flees from the hellish hags of remorse that pursue him to his death."

> "While music flows around
> Perfumes and oils and wine and wanton hours,
> Amid the roses fierce Repentance rears
> Her snaky crest."
>
> (Thomson's "Seasons," Spring, l. 994.)

The teaching of this section is as true now as it ever was.   True of individuals now as in Job's time.   True of our nation as of the Jews.   And we should take warning from their experience—Israel destroyed at Samaria; Judah carried captive with city and temple swept out of existence; the Jews who lost city and temple by the Romans as Christ himself foretold.   Job's lesson is for all.

PART III

THE INTERVENTION OF ELIHU. POETRY. (Chapters XXXII–XXXVII.)

THIRD SOLUTION: THAT SUFFERING IS A MEANS OF DISCIPLINE EVEN WHEN SENT OR PERMITTED ALSO FOR OTHER ENDS, AS FOR A TEST OR A PUNISHMENT

RESEARCH QUESTIONS

(To be assigned to different members of the class at the previous session, and for class discussion.)

1. Review of the subject up to this time.
2. Elihu; who he was; why introduced into the poem.
3. Character of Elihu, as learned from his address.
4. The purpose and aim of his address.
5. Specially interesting particulars in it.
6. Why is suffering of some kind necessary to a perfect character?
7. How far is the punishment of sin intended also for a discipline?
8. Is there any difference, as to educational value, between sufferings that come upon us from outward causes, and those which come upon us through our conflicts with evil?
9. Illustrate from the Exile and its effects upon the Jewish nation.
10. Find other instances in the Old Testament.
11. Find instances in the New Testament.
12. In what ways was Jesus made "perfect through suffering"? (Heb. iii. 10, 18; iv. 15; v. 8.)
13. Hymns bearing upon this subject.
14. Illustrations from history, literature, and experience.

BLACKBOARD

INTRODUCTION OF ELIHU : xxxii. 1–5.
Prose. All the rest in Poetry.

AUDIENCE : Job, Eliphaz, Bildad, Zophar, neighbors,
citizens.

SCENE : A mound of ashes, outside the walls.

PRELUDE : Of Elihu's speech. xxxii. 6–22.
(To the Friends.)

1ST DIVISION : Ch. xxxiii.
(To Job.)
*(Job makes no sign.   Elihu turns to the
Friends.)*

2ND DIVISION : Ch. xxxiv.
(To the three Friends.)
(They give no sign.)

3RD DIVISION : Ch. xxxv.
(To Job and the Friends.)

4TH DIVISION : Chs. xxxvi, xxxvii.
(General Application.)

During this part of Elihu's speech, *there are signs of the
coming of a storm, with increasing violence; preparing for
the Voice from the Whirlwind.* (xxxvi. 27–xxxvii. 24.)

THE INTRODUCTION OF ELIHU. (Job xxxii. 1–5.)
In Prose, by the author.

ELIHU was a young man who had been present during the previous discussion. His name means "He is my God." The Jews were accustomed to give names with a meaning, as the Puritans used to, and the Indians do to this day. "Among the names of the Monks who subscribed to the Act of Surrender in 1540, are those of **Charity, Faith, Godhaps,** and **Godluck.**" (George G. Bradley, D.D., "Lectures on Job," p. 285, note.) Elihu belonged to the family of Buz, a brother of Uz, a descendant of Nahor, the brother of Abraham (compare Gen. xxii. 21, 22 with Jer. xxv. 23), dwelling near Dedan in Arabia. He was an Aramean (Syrian) of the family or tribe of Ram = Aram = Syria. (2 Chr. xxiii. 5.) He was a worshipper of one God, but not an Israelite.

Something of his personal appearance we may learn from Jer. xxv. 29, where the Buzites are said to have the corners of their hair polled (i. e., cut short) all around their temples; because, like Paul, they thought it a shame for a man to wear long hair. So Herodotus (iii. 8) describes the Arabs as cutting their hair à la Bacchus, i. e., in a ring away from their temples.

Elihu had the natural tendencies of youth; not a "pert, braggart boy," not "a most conceited and arrogant young man," but with the self-confidence and dogmatism of one who has never been tried with great affliction. He had something of the assurance of a sea captain who has studied navigation, but has not weathered mighty storms; of a cadet thoroughly versed in military science, but who has not yet led great armies in battle.

Elihu "occupies the position of a young man intervening uninvited in a debate of old men. With the almost superstitious reverence for old age that belongs to early civilizations, it is natural to find that Elihu has great difficulty in nerving himself to this effort; and it takes him fifty-two lines to complete his apology for speaking at all in so venerable a presence." (See Moulton, "Modern Reader's Bible," xxix, xxx.)

Many scholars think that Elihu's discourses were no part of the original Book of Job, but the strongest arguments for that view are really arguments for its being a part of the original complete poem.

The difference in the language from that of the other speakers, being full of Aramaisms, is really the natural effect of his being an Aramite.

Cheyne thinks his speech interrupts the connection between the words of Job and the words of Jehovah out of the storm. But one of the most beautiful and poetic as well as most natural portions of the whole book is that wonderful conception of the coming of the storm during Elihu's speech.

It is said that Elihu adds nothing to what the Friends have said. But he does bring out into clear, shining vision, what the Friends only hinted at, the hints also being obscured by the passionate trend of their argument. The poem and its solution would have been incomplete without Elihu's part in it.

ELIHU'S SPEECHES.—While all through his four discourses, or heads of a single discourse, Elihu refers to mistaken utterances of Job, to things said by him in the surging turmoil of his agony and conflict, and which do not represent the outcome of this inner warfare of the soul, yet his main contribution to the progressive solution of the problem of suffering lies in his emphasis on the fact that God is disciplining his children and leading them upward to a higher, sweeter, nobler life.

THE READINGS will be confined chiefly to these portions of his discourse, with their necessary setting.

ELIHU (chapter xxxii). (*Opening remarks to the audience, especially the three* FRIENDS.)

I am young,
   And ye are very old;
Wherefore I held back,
   And durst not shew you mine opinion.
I said, Days should speak,
   And multitude of years should teach wisdom.
   But there is a spirit in man,
   And the breath of the Almighty giveth them understanding.
It is not the great that are wise,
   Nor the aged that understand judgment.
   Therefore I say, Hearken to me;
   I also will shew mine opinion.
   For I am full of words;
Like new bottles it is ready to burst.[1]

FIRST DIVISION (chapter xxxiii). (*Turning to Job.*)

Howbeit, Job, I pray thee, hear my speech,
   And hearken to all my words.
Surely thou hast spoken in mine hearing,
   And I have heard the voice of thy words, saying,
      "I am clean without transgression;
      "I am innocent, neither is there iniquity in me:"[2]
      "He counteth me for his enemy."

---

[1] Job xxxii. 6–10, 18, 19. Marg. for last line, "bottles which are ready to burst." Skin bottles filled with fermenting wine. Compare Matt. ix. 17.
[2] Verbally true, but not the complete statement of Job's feelings.

God speaketh once,
Yea twice, though man regardeth it not.

In a dream, in a vision of the night,
When deep sleep falleth upon men,
In slumberings upon the bed;

Then he openeth the ears of men,
And sealeth their instruction,
That he may withdraw man from his purpose,
And hide pride from man;
He keepeth back his soul from the pit,
And his life from perishing by the sword.

He is chastened also with pain upon his bed,
So that his life abhorreth bread,
Yea, his soul draweth near unto the pit,
And his life to the destroyers.

If there be with him an angel,
An interpreter, one among a thousand,
To shew unto man what is right for him;
Then he is gracious unto him, and saith,
"Deliver him from going down to the pit,
I have found a ransom."

His flesh shall be fresher than a child's;
He returneth to the days of his youth:
He prayeth unto God,[1]
And he is favourable unto him;
So that he seeth his face with joy:
And he restoreth unto man his righteousness.
He singeth before men, and saith,[2]

---

[1] The Ancient Mariner first could pray when he began to love God's creatures.

[2] Songs of redemption, Rev. v. 9; xv. 3; Ps. xcviii. 1. The joy of the Lord, John xvii. 3; Acts ii. 46; Phil. iv. 4.

"I have sinned, and perverted that which was right,
And it profited me not:
He hath redeemed my soul from going into the pit,
And my life shall behold the light."

**Lo, all these things doth God work,
Twice, yea thrice, with a man;
To bring back his soul from the pit,
That he may be enlightened with the light of the living.**

Mark well, O Job, hearken unto me
If thou hast anything to say, answer me:
Speak, for I desire to justify thee.[1]

(*He looks to* JOB: JOB *makes no sign.*)

SECOND DIVISION (chapter xxxiv). (*He turns to the three* FRIENDS.)

Hear my words, ye wise men.
Let us know among ourselves what is good.
For Job has said "I am righteous,
And God hath taken away my right."
For he hath said, "It profiteth a man nothing
That he should delight himself with God."
Far be it from God, that he should do wickedness;
And from the Almighty, that he should commit iniquity.
Is it fit
To say to a king, Thou art vile?
Or to nobles, Ye are wicked?
How much less
To him that respecteth not the persons of princes,
Nor regardeth the rich more than the poor.
For hath any said unto God,
**" I have borne chastisement,
I will not offend any more:** [2]

---

[1] Job xxxiii. 1, 8-10, 14-20, 22-32.
[2] Margin, "though I offend not."

That which I see not teach thou me:
If I have done iniquity, I will do it no more?"
Job speaketh without knowledge.[1]

(ELIHU looks to the three FRIENDS: they give no sign.)

THIRD DIVISION (chapter xxxv).   (To JOB and his three FRIENDS.)
LOOK UNTO THE HEAVENS, AND SEE;
And behold the skies, which are higher than thou.

If thou hast sinned,
    What doest thou against him?
And if thy transgressions be multiplied,
    What doest thou unto him?
If thou be righteous,
    What givest thou him?

But none saith, "**Where is God my Maker,**
Who giveth songs in the night;[2]
Who teacheth us more than the beasts of the earth,
And maketh us wiser than the fowls of heaven?"[3]

FOURTH DIVISION (chapters xxxvi, xxxvii).

(General expression of his thoughts.)

Suffer me a little, and I will show thee.
If they be bound in fetters,
And be taken in the cords of affliction;
    Then he showeth them their work and their transgressions
    That they have behaved themselves proudly.
He openeth also their ear to instruction,
And commandeth that they return from inquity.
If they hearken and serve him,
    They shall spend their days in prosperity,
    And their years in pleasure.[4]

---

[1] Job xxxiv. 2, 4, 5, 9, 10, 18, 19, 31, 32, 35.
[2] Paul and Silas singing songs in the night, Acts xvi. 25; Madame Guyon's Prison Song, "A little bird I am." See Peloubet's " Suggestive Illustrations on the Acts," pp. 338, 339.
[3] Job xxxv. 5-7, 10-11.
[4] Margin—" pleasantness."

Yea, he would have led thee away out of distress
Into a broad place, where there is no straitness.[1]

(The portion of ELIHU'S *speech in which he notices the coming of the storm will be considered under the introduction to the Theophany.)*

THE OUTCOME.—"If we weave these three lines of thought into a single argument, it may be doubted whether even now that we hold the added thought and experience of some thirty centuries at our service, the most searching and inquisitive intellect can make any real addition to this ancient solution of the great problem of human life and thought. For when we have said that under the just and kindly providence of God good comes to the good and evil to the evil and unthankful; that the very sufferings imposed on men, whether they be the natural results of their own transgression, or the strokes of a merciful and fruitful discipline, are intended for their instruction, correction and redemption; and that whatever wrongs are not remedied here shall be remedied hereafter, and whatever undeserved sufferings produce no present fruit of happiness shall bear a richer harvest in the world to come; when we have said all this, what more or better have even the wisest of us to say?" (Samuel Cox, "Commentary on Job," pp. 87–88.)

THIRD SOLUTION

Another reason for suffering lies in the fact that it is one of the Exercises in the School of Life, by which we are educated and trained in heavenly character and usefulness.

THE SCHOOL OF LIFE.—In the making of a man or a nation it has been the universal experience that pain, disappointment, conflicts with temptation, have been among the means God has used. They have been among God's schoolmasters to teach and train his people.

In the cemetery among the beautiful hills of Williamstown stands a monument to one of my college classmates. While wrestling, in his freshman year, he injured his knee. Lameness, pain, and ill-health were his guardian angels through study and travel, till he became a professor in the college and a saintly man, whose face shone almost like that of Moses when he came from the presence of God. On that monument are carved the words which his life had wrought out: *Meine Trübsal war mein Glück*, "My misfortune has been my good fortune," "My trouble has been my blessing."

Almost every one who has grown in grace has learned the truth of that Greek proverb, old as Herodotus and Æschylus, *Ta pathemata mathemata*, The things we have experienced, our burdens, our difficulties, our struggles, our sufferings, are the things that teach us.

Job xxxvi. 2, 8–12, 16.

TRIBULATION.—Archbishop Trench in his "Study of Words" (pp. 38–40) illustrates this word "which occurs not seldom in Scripture and in the [Church of England] Liturgy. It means affliction, sorrow, anguish; but it is quite worth our while to know *how* it means this, and to question 'tribulation' a little closer. It is derived from the Latin 'tribulum,' which was the threshing instrument or harrow whereby the Roman husbandman separated the corn from the husks, and 'tribulatio' in its primary significance of the act was this separation."

"So far as to the primitive figure of speech. But some Latin writer of the Christian Church appropriated the word and image for the setting forth of a higher truth; and sorrow, distress, and adversity being the appointed means for the separating in men of whatever in them was light, trivial, and poor, from the solid and the true, their chaff from their wheat, he therefore called these sorrows and trials 'tribulations'—threshings, that is, of the inner spiritual man, without which there could be no fitting him for the heavenly garner." It is also said, as to this signification: "This deeper religious use of the word 'tribulation' was unknown to classical antiquity, belonging exclusively to the Christian writers."

Trench quotes, in illustration of this truth, the following lines by "George Wither, a prolific versifier, and occasionally a poet, of the seventeenth century."

> "Till from the straw the flail the corn doth beat,
> Until the chaff be purgèd from the wheat,
> Yea, till the mill the grains in pieces tear,
> The richness of the flour will scarce appear.
> So, till men's persons great afflictions touch,
> If worth be found, their worth is not so much,
> Because, like wheat in straw, they have not yet
> That value which in threshing they may get.
> For till the bruising flails of God's corrections
> Have threshèd out of us our vain affections;
> Till those corrections which do misbecome us
> Are by thy sacred Spirit winnowed from us;
> Until from us the straw of worldly treasures,
> Till all the dusty chaff of empty pleasures,
> Yea, till his flail upon us he doth lay,
> To thresh the husk of this our flesh away;
> And leave the soul uncovered; nay, yet more,
> Till God shall make our very spirit poor,
> We shall not up to highest wealth aspire;
> But then we shall; and that is my desire."

The emphasis is not on the threshing, but on the grain; not on the chastisement, but on the character that results.

DISCIPLINE means teaching, education, training, causing the disciple-learner, one who goes to school—to learn the qualities and character which make heaven.

CHASTISEMENT is derived from "chasten," "to make chaste," "and 'chaste' is the beautiful, snowy Latin 'castus,' spotless, pure, holy," whiter than snow.

God disciplines far more by good than by evil, by the blessings of life than by its sorrows, by the long prosperous years of Job before and after his tribulations than by his sufferings. But he used and uses both.

While persecution and trouble develop certain virtues, there are others which are developed better in times of peace. Disciples need both kinds of training. Night is necessary as well as day, but all darkness is even more disastrous than all daytime.

Jeremy Taylor describes some lamps in the tomb of Terentia as burning brightly in the darkness of the tomb, but going out when brought forth into the light, as a type of Christians whose piety burns brightly in the darkness of persecution and trouble, but goes out in the light of prosperity. Mr. Rogers, commenting on this, says that it by no means follows that all darkness is good for the Christian, for " then the bright lamps of which Taylor speaks would irradiate only a tomb."

THE QUARRY FOR THE TEMPLE.—This world is a quarry where the living stones of God's beautiful temple in the heavens, the completed and perfected church, are being shaped and polished for their places in the building. Few places are more rough, more lacking in every element of beauty, than a stone quarry. I began my ministry among the quarries of Cape Ann, which have since been multiplying over its granite surface. Were I to take the owners of some of the newer quarries and walk with them over the familiar places, I could say to them: "I remember when I used to walk here among stately trees, or sit under the shadow of a great rock and feast on the surrounding beauties; but now you have blasted the rocks, you have cut down the trees, you have littered the fields with broken fragments. What does it all mean?" Then they could take me to some noble buildings in various cities and say: "Do you see those stately buildings, beautiful cornices, graceful arches, lofty columns? Well, there is the meaning of the quarry." So the heavenly temple is the solution of the mysteries of Providence in this world. The cares, burdens, sorrows, joys, work of this life are fitting us for our place in that temple where no sound of the tools shall be heard while it is in building.

There is a story, told in the " Choir Boy of York Cathedral," of a man named Theodorus who went to Athens and fell asleep in the temple of Minerva. He dreamed that he went to another place where there was a Palace of Destiny. This was in the form of a pyramid. Each story represented a world. Theodorus saw a friend of his, called Sextus, in each one of these stories, or worlds. In one world he was prosperous and good; in another he was contented with a very humble lot; in still another he was a king, and a good king, too. Finally, Theodorus entered the highest apartment of all, and was so delighted that he nearly fainted for joy. But here he saw Sextus, a wicked man and ruined forever. "This," said his guide, "is the very best world of all"; but Theodorus was puzzled to know how it could be the best and yet make his friend Sextus worse off in it than in any of the others. "It is the best possible world," said his guide, "and Sextus might have made the best out of it." "The best possible world" is best only for those who have learned to love and obey God perfectly. Adam was driven from Paradise because it was not the best place for him. A world of discipline is the best then. But when men are fully redeemed from sin then they can also dwell in Paradise Regained, the glorious city of God.

"In the Arabian Nights' tales there is a story of a remarkable ointment which, if rubbed on the eye, makes one see all the riches in the world; the gold hidden in the mines; the diamonds treasured in secret places. Macaulay, the great English writer, said that education is like that ointment, opening the eyes to see so much more." (President Seth Low, in an address on Education.)

This is especially true of the moral education which comes through the divine training and discipline.

Charles Mackay has a poem in which Milton, blind to the blue sky, "sees the bowers of Paradise"; and Beethoven, "Music's Great High Priest," deaf to all sound, yet in his soul hears "jubilant hymns and lays of love."

"To blind old Milton's rayless orbs
A light divine is given,
And deaf Beethoven hears the hymns
And harmonies of heaven."

"And when a damp
Fell round the path of Milton, in his hand
The Thing became a trumpet, whence he blew
Soul-animating strains—alas, too few."
(Wordsworth, " Scorn not the Sonnet.")

"All God's angels come to us disguised;
Sorrow and sickness, poverty and death,
One after other lift their frowning masks,
And we behold the seraph's face beneath
All radiant with the glory and the calm
Of having looked upon the front of God."
(J. R. Lowell, " On the Death of a Friend's Child.")

See Ugo Bassi's "Sermon in the Hospital"; Bushnell's " Moral Uses of Dark Things"; Peloubet's " Loom of Life."

Note that often small trials constantly repeated are often more difficult to bear than some great trouble. It is less easy to endure the buzz and bite of a cloud of mosquito troubles than the lion roar of a great affliction. Hence the petty annoyances, the frettings of temper, the daily and hourly trials are often the means of our severest and most effective discipline.

Tennyson says ("In Memoriam," i):

> "I held it truth, with him who sings
> To one clear harp in divers tones,
> That men may rise on stepping-stones
> Of their dead selves to higher things."

But it is far better to rise on stepping-stones of their *living* selves to higher things. If, as Longfellow says (in his "Ladder of St. Augustine"),

> "Of our vices we can frame
> A ladder, if we will but tread
> Beneath our feet each deed of shame,"

how much more can we frame a ladder of all deeds faithfully done:

> "Arise and fly
> The reeling faun, the sensual feast;
> Move upward, working out the beast,
> And let the ape and tiger die."
> (Tennyson, "In Memoriam," cxviii.)

Conflicts, hard duties, self-sacrifices, are the means of making men. The father who shelters his boy from these is doing his best to ruin him.

Governor Seymour, of New York, once said that if God should give him the opportunity to live his life over again, and to choose which of the things in the life he had lived he would retain and which he would leave out, whatever other changes he might make, he would not dare to leave out a single trial or hard duty.

We dream of Edens without care or annoyance or pain; we join in the wish of the poet:

> "O could we do with this world of ours
> As thou dost with thy garden bowers,
> Reject the weeds and keep the flowers,
> What a heaven on earth we'd make it!"
> (Thomas Moore, "Lalla Rookh.")

But God always casts us out of these Eden dreams. For the fallen Adam and Eve Eden was the worst place in the world. God drove them out that they might attain to Paradise Regained.

The meaning of burdens, cares, sorrows, is nobler and purer lives, sweeter harps, brighter crowns, higher thrones.

Compare Johnson's "Rasselas" in the Happy Valley; Professor James's experience at Chautauqua, in his "Talks to Teachers on Psychology," pp. 268–75.

Compare the Seven Promises to him that overcometh, in Revelation ii., iii. And Christ's example in the Wilderness of temptation, and in Gethsemane, as interpreted in Hebrews ii. 16–18; iii. 10, 18; iv. 15; v. 8; and the power of sympathy and help he gained on those battlefields, or perhaps rather we gain from knowing his experience.

In the same way we gain a similar power in our degree of comforting and helping others, one of the richest blessings ever conferred on man.

The Exile of the Jews teaches us a lesson. For their sins they were sent into long and terrible exile, homes and nation destroyed, organized worship in the temple no longer possible, Sabbath almost impossible under heathen masters. But there they learned the lesson of the evil of disobedience and unrighteousness. They came to hunger and thirst after God's worship and Word, and thus became prepared to return and build up the nation anew. The New Jerusalem will be the fulfilment of their vision and hope.

> "All thoughts of ill; all evil deeds,
>   That have their root in thoughts of ill;
> Whatever hinders or impedes
>   The action of the nobler will—
>
> "All these must first be trampled down
>   Beneath our feet, if we would gain
> In the bright fields of fair renown
>   The right of eminent domain."
>   (Longfellow, "Ladder of St. Augustine.")

All the fruits of the Spirit are ripened by conflict with the works of the flesh and victory over them.

We learn joy by conquering the false joys of the world, by triumph over sorrow.

We learn love by victory over the enemies that hate us.

We learn peace by clinging to Christ in the storm.

We learn faithfulness by duties done when to do them means hardship and loss.

We learn kindness by doing good to them that hate us and despitefully use us.

We learn temperance by victory over our strong appetites and passions.

We learn meekness and patience in an evil world, full of wrongs.

"Build thee more stately mansions,
    Oh, my soul,
As the swift seasons roll!
Leave thy low-vaulted past!
Let each new temple, nobler than the last,
Shut thee from heaven with a dome more vast,
    Till thou at length art free,
Leaving thine outworn shell by life's unresting sea."
        (O. W. Holmes, " The Chambered Nautilus.")

And thou shalt remember all the way which the Lord thy God led thee these forty years in the wilderness, to humble thee, and to prove thee, to know what was in thine heart, whether thou wouldest keep his commandments, or no. (Deut. viii. 2.)

PART IV

THE VOICE OF GOD FROM THE WHIRL-WIND. (Chapters xxxviii. 1–xlii. 6.)

FOURTH SOLUTION: THERE ARE SOME TROUBLES WHICH ARE AN INSOLUBLE MYSTERY, BUT GOD HAS REVEALED HIMSELF AS SO GOOD, SO WISE, SO POWERFUL, SUCH A LOVING FATHER, THAT WE CAN REST OUR SOULS ON HIM IN PERFECT PEACE AND FAITH AND LOVE

RESEARCH QUESTIONS

(To be assigned to various members of the class at the previous session, and for general discussion.)

1. The poetic beauty and effectiveness of the approach of the storm.

2. What kinds of suffering and evil are an inscrutable mystery?

3. The appropriateness of God's speaking from a whirlwind.   John iii. 5–8; Acts ii. 1–4.

4. The use of nature by Christ in his teachings.   What things in nature he uses, and their teachings.

5. The value of studying nature in this way in our religious education.

6. Why is nature a symbol and illustration of spiritual truths?

7. What do we learn concerning God's wisdom from nature?

8. What do we learn concerning his power?

9. What concerning his goodness?

10. How does nature lead us to faith in God, as a help and comfort in trouble?

11. Why do we need the revelation of Jesus Christ in order to understand God in his fulness, and in order to fully trust him?

12. Effect of this vision of God upon Job.

13. Hymns concerning nature as revealing God.

14. Illustrations from literature and experience.

79

PREPARATIONS FOR THE VOICE OF GOD

(Beginning at xxxvi. 26, at which point signs of an approaching storm appear in the sky, which gradually increase in intensity during the remainder of ELIHU'S *speech, which seems to have been cut short by the overwhelming force of the storm.)*

SCENE.—JOB, *his* FRIENDS, ELIHU, *and bystanders, are all upon or around the great ash mound outside of the city, exposed to the full force of the storm.* ELIHU *was probably speaking from the top of the mound whence he could see the skies in every direction.*

READINGS.[1]

ELIHU (chapters xxxvi. 26–xxxvii. 24).

Behold, God is great, and we know him not;
The number of his years is unsearchable.

(The sun drawing water.)

For he draweth up the drops of water,
Which distil in rain from his vapor:

(A shower in the distance.)

Which the skies pour down
And drop upon man abundantly.

(Distant thunder.)

Yea, can any understand the spreadings of the clouds,
The thunderings of his pavilion?
Behold, he spreadeth his light around him;
And he covereth the bottom of the sea.
For by these he judgeth the peoples;
He giveth meat in abundance.

(Lightning bolt from clouds to earth.)

He covereth his hands with the lightning;
And giveth it a charge that it strike the mark.
The noise thereof telleth concerning him,
The cattle also concerning the storm that cometh up.

(A loud peal of thunder, close at hand.)

---

[1] Moulton and Cary best set forth the coming of the storm, and I follow their general lines of expressing its progress.

At this also my heart trembleth,
And is moved out of its place.
Hearken ye unto the noise of his voice,
And the sound that goeth out of his mouth.

(Thunder and lightning all around the horizon.)

He sendeth it forth under the whole heaven,
And his lightning unto the ends of the earth.
After it a voice roareth;
    He thundereth with the voice of his majesty:
And he stayeth them not when his voice is heard.

(The storm increases.)

God thundereth marvellously with his voice;
Great things doeth he, which we cannot comprehend.

(Hail and snow.)

For he saith to the snow, Fall thou on the earth;
    Likewise to the shower of rain,
    And to the showers of his mighty rain.

(The storm increases in violence.)

Then the beasts go into coverts,
    And remain in their dens.

(The warm storm from the south meets the
cold one from the north.)

Out of the chamber of the south cometh the storm:
    And cold out of the north.
By the breath of God ice is given:
    And the breadth of the waters is straitened.[1]
Yea, he ladeth the thick cloud with moisture;
He spreadeth abroad the cloud of his lightning:

(The storm has become a whirlwind; the
whole scene is wrapped in thick dark-
ness, broken by flashes of lightning.)

And it is turned round about by his guidance,
That they may do whatsoever he commandeth them

[1] Margin, "congealed."

Upon the face of the habitable world:
Whether it be for correction, or for his land,
Or for mercy, that he cause it to come.
Hearken unto this, O Job:
Stand still, and consider the wondrous works of God.

Dost thou know how God layeth his charge upon them,
And causeth the lightning of his cloud to shine?
Dost thou know the balancings of the clouds,[1]
    The wondrous works of him which is perfect in knowledge?

> (*A change to sultry heat which precedes the
> coming of the cyclone.*)

How thy garments are warm
When the earth is still by reason of the south wind.
Canst thou with him spread out the sky,
    Which is strong as a molten mirror?
Teach us what we shall say unto him;
    For we cannot order our speech by reason of darkness.[2]

> (*The storm cloud has now plunged them in
> its thickest darkness, filling* ELIHU *with
> terror.*)

Shall it be told him that I would speak?
Or should a man wish that he were swallowed up?[3]

> (*Supernatural brightness too vivid to gaze
> upon mingles strangely with the dark-
> ness of the storm.*)

And now men see not the light which is bright in the skies;
But the wind passeth and cleanseth them.[4]
Out of the north cometh golden splendor:

> (*The Shekinah, the manifestation of Jeho-
> vah's visible presence, shining upon the
> dark background of the storm cloud.*)

---

[1] See Ruskin, "Modern Painters," vol. v, "The cloud-chariots."

[2] Elihu's succeeding words, accordingly, are confused and incoherent, indicating a vague terror of impending destruction. (Genung, p. 325.)

[3] Margin, "If a man speak surely he shall be swallowed up."

[4] Margin, "And now men cannot look on the light when it is bright in the skies, when the wind hath passed, and cleansed them."

God hath upon him terrible majesty.
Touching the Almighty, we cannot find him out; he is excellent
  in power;
And in judgment and plenteous justice he will not afflict.
Men do therefore fear him:
He regardeth not any that are wise of heart.

> (*The roar of the whirlwind gives place to*
> *a* VOICE.)

No portion of the poem is more poetic and dramatic in form than this commingling with exquisite tact and skill Elihu's closing argument with the description of the approaching storm.

With the 22d verse "Elihu begins to retract his pretensions, and in a kind
of wheedling terror to bring God's mercies to mind, as if in a confused attempt
thereby to turn away the wrath that seems so imminent.

" This is the last of Elihu. He is self-judged. Though he has said many
noble things, and represented the highest and the truest that the friends could
bring forth from the treasures of their Wisdom, yet, because of its unspiritual
and essentially selfish basis in their character, it does not enable them to stand
before the searching light of God's immediate presence. It is only aspiring love
and purity of heart that can endure His face." (Genung, " Epic of the Inner
Life," p. 326.)

Compare Lord Marmion's experience in Walter Scott's poem, when a word,
a look from the reverend palmer, "full upon his conscience struck."

> "Thus oft it haps that, when within
>   They shrink at sense of secret sin,
>   A feather daunts the brave,
>   A fool's wild speech confounds the wise,
>   And proudest princes veil their eyes
>   Before their meanest slave."

THE GOLDEN SPLENDOR.—The "north" from which came the golden
splendor " must not be taken of the north wind cleansing the skies, but of the
north as in prophetic imagination the quarter specially associated with the
Divine abode, or the direction from which the God of Judgment makes his
appearance. This is perfectly clear from *Isaiah*, chapter xiv. 13:
  '*Sit upon the mount of congregation, in the uttermost parts of the north: I
will ascend above the heights of the clouds; I will be like the Most High.*'
  ' (Compare *Ezekiel*, chapter i. 4; *Jeremiah*, vi. 1; i. 13–14, etc.) It is a regular
feature of the theophanies of Scripture to have a supernatural brightness as a
stage beyond the natural tempest. Thus in Ezekiel's vision (i. 4):

'*Behold, a stormy wind came out of the north, a great cloud, with a fire flash-ing continually, and a brightness round about it*,' etc." (Moulton, "Modern Reader's Bible," p. 175.)

Note that the manifestation of God is through the two symbols which best express the nature of God—Light and Wind.

THE SHEKINAH, the visible expression of God's presence among the children of Israel, was seen in the flaming bush; in the pillar of cloud and fire (Ex. xiii. 21, 22); on Mt. Sinai at the giving of the law, like "a devouring fire in the eyes of the children of Israel" (Ex. xxiv. 10-17); filling the Tabernacle (Ex. xl. 34, 35); and the Temple at its dedication (1 Kin. xiii. 10, 11; 2 Chron. vii. 1-3).

Physical science declares that there is "an intangible, invisible ether, which cannot be touched or tasted or contained or measured or weighed, but yet *is* everywhere, and in one form or another does all the physical work of the universe." Light is one kind of motion in this ether. Yet "it is invisible, inconceivable, unknown to us, *unless* matter to make it visible is in its path." (See Lewis Wright, "Light," chap. xviii.)

Light is mysterious in its nature, ineffably bright and glorious, everywhere present, swift-winged, undefiled, and undefilable. Light is the source of life, of beauty, of manifested reality, of warmth, comfort, and joy, of health, and of power. It destroys all darkness; it unites in itself purity and clearness. Without it the world would be but a mass of coldness and death.

THE WHIRLWIND.—Nothing is more suitable than that the voice of God should come from the whirlwind. For (1) Air, wind, is one of the chosen symbols of God working through his Holy Spirit, as at Pentecost. The same Greek word signifies both spirit and wind. (See John iii. 5-8; Acts ii. 1-4, etc.)

It is invisible, as are the great natural forces of the earth.

It is known by its works, by what it does.

It is mysterious, no one knows whence it comes or whither it goes. No Weather Bureau knows why or whence. It can only observe and report its movements.

It is very powerful. The air is so powerful that even free dynamite smiting against it on one side crushes the rocks on the other.

Yet it is very gentle and delicate, breathing around the rose, and gently touching the little child.

It comes pure from heaven.

The air is all-pervasive. It penetrates the hardest rock.

It is the breath of life. No one can live without it.

(2) The storm was a symbol of the afflictions of Job. All its manifestations as described above, coming so mysteriously, expressed the storm that had swept over his soul.

I know of nothing which sets out the scene so vividly as the experience of Elijah on Horeb.

"On Horeb's rock the prophet stood,
The Lord before him passed;
A hurricane in angry mood
Swept by him strong and fast.

The forests fell before its force
The rocks were shivered in its course.
.   .   .   .   .   .
'Twas but the whirlwind of his breath
Announcing danger, wreck and death.
.   .   .   .
'Twas but the rolling of his car
The trampling of his steeds afar.
.   .   .   .
At last a voice all still and small
Rose sweetly on the ear,
Yet rose so shrill and clear that all
In heaven and earth might hear.

It spoke of peace, it spoke of love,
It spoke as angels speak above,
And God himself was here;
For oh, it was a Father's voice
That made the trembling world rejoice."
                                    (Henry F. Lyte.)

THE VOICE FROM THE WHIRLWIND. (Job xxxviii. 2–xl. 6.)

THE LORD.
Who is this that darkeneth counsel
By words without knowledge?
Gird up now thy loins like a man;
For I will demand of thee, and declare thou unto me.

Where wast thou when I laid the foundations of the earth?
—Declare, if thou hast understanding—
Who determined the measures thereof, if thou knowest?
Or who stretched the line upon it?
Whereupon were the foundations thereof fastened?
Or who laid the corner stone thereof;

When the morning stars sang together,
And all the sons of God shouted for joy?
Or who shut up the sea with doors,
And prescribed for it my decree,
And set bars and doors,
And said, Hitherto shalt thou come, but no further;
And here shall thy proud waves be stayed?

Hast thou entered into the springs of the sea?
Or hast thou walked in the recesses of the deep?

Have the gates of death been revealed unto thee?
Hast thou entered the treasuries of the snow,
Or hast thou seen the treasuries of the hail,
Canst thou bind the cluster of the Pleiades,
Or loose the bands of Orion?
Canst thou lead forth the Mazzaroth [1] in their season?
Or canst thou guide the Bear with her train?
Canst thou send forth lightnings, that they may go,
And say unto thee, Here we are?

Shall he that cavilleth contend with the Almighty?
He that argueth with God, let him answer it. [2]

(A lull in the storm.)

JOB.

Behold, I am of small account; what shall I answer thee?
I lay mine hand upon my mouth.
Once have I spoken, and I will not answer;
Yea twice, but I will proceed no further. [3]

(The whirlwind awakens again.)

THE LORD (chapters xl. 7-xli. 34). *(Speaking out of the whirlwind. We must consider that the thunderstorm is still raging.)*

Gird up thy loins now like a man:
I will demand of thee, and declare thou unto me.

---

[1] Margin, "the signs of the Zodiac."
[2] Job xxxviii. 2-8, 10, 11, 16, 17, 22, 31, 32, 35; xl. 2
[3] Job xl. 4, 5.

Wilt thou even disannul my judgment?
  Wilt thou condemn me, that thou mayest be justified?
  Or hast thou an arm like God?
  And canst thou thunder with a voice like him?
Deck thyself now with excellency and dignity;
  And array thyself with honor and majesty.
Pour forth the overflowings of thine anger:
  And look upon every one that is proud, and abase him.
  And tread down the wicked where they stand.
Hide them in the dust together;
  Bind their faces in the hidden place.
Then will I also confess of thee
That thine own right hand can save thee.

Behold now behemoth,[1] which I made with thee;
  Shall any take him when he is on the watch,
  Or pierce through his nose with a snare?
Canst thou draw out leviathan [2] with a fish-hook?
  Or press down his tongue with a cord?
    Lay thine hand upon him;
    Remember the battle,
    And do so no more.
                              (*The storm begins to abate.*)

JOB.

  I know that thou canst do all things,
  And that no purpose of thine can be restrained.

THE LORD.[3]

  Who is this that hideth counsel without knowledge?
                              (*The* VOICE *retreating.*)

JOB.

  Therefore have I uttered that which I understood not,
  Things too wonderful for me, which I knew not.
  Hear, I beseech thee, and I will speak.
                              (*More distant.*)

---

[1] The hippopotamus.
[2] The crocodile.
[3] These divisions are made by Moulton. This saying is a quotation of God's word concerning Elihu (xxxviii. 2.) Either the Lord repeats it or Job quotes it to apply it.

THE LORD.[1]

> I will demand of thee, and declare thou unto me.

JOB.

> **I had heard of thee by the hearing of the ear;**
> **But now mine eye seeth thee:**
> **Wherefore I abhor myself,**
> **And repent in dust and ashes.**[2]

> *(The storm ceases.)*

"The treasuries of the snow," (xxxviii. 22.)   Many are the uses of snow in the economy of nature; the treasure-house of water for spring, the blanket that keeps plant life from freezing to death.   For its power recall the armies of Napoleon on their retreat from Moscow.   See Natural Philosophies; " Snowflakes "; McCook's " The Gospel in Nature," Snow Crystals, Purity of Snow, and several other chapters on snow.

"Contend with the Almighty," (xl. 2.)   "Because there is sin and misery in the world, because hearts ache and bodies die, shall we turn upon this sublimely exhaustless Being, and demand explanation?   Is it not something to know how He delights in making, in endless creating, and that One who thus delights cannot be cruel?   The explanation will come." (Robert Buchanan.)

On the meaning and power of nature, especially the sea, the clouds and sky, and the mountains, see Ruskin's " Modern Painters," vol. v, which gave me a new revelation of nature.

Dr. Amory H. Bradford's " Messages of the Masters," chapters on Giron's The Mountains, the grandeur and glory of the mountains; on Renouf's The Pilot, the message and ministry of the sea; and on Turner's The Old Temeraire, the mystery and ministry of the sea.

Hugh MacMillan's " Bible Teachings in Nature "; Coleridge's " Hymn to Mont Blanc "; H. C. McCook's " The Gospel in Nature "; Dr. E. F. Burr's " Ecce Cœlum "; Agnes Giberne's " The Stars."   The little book " The Stars and the Earth " is very remarkable.   Study the allusions to nature in the Psalms, especially Psalms xix and cvii, and in Isaiah and the other prophets.

---

[1] This too is a quotation of God's words to Job (xxxviii. 3) or a repetition by the Lord.
[2] Job xl. 7–15, 24; xli. 1, 8; xlii. 2–6.

THE FOURTH SOLUTION

IN THE FIRST PLACE, recall the fact that there are sorrows and pains which are an insoluble mystery. In every life there are losses and disappointments and sickness and death for which we can see no reason.

> "There is no flock however watched and tended
> But one dead lamb is there,
> There is no fireside howsoe'er defended
> But has one vacant chair.

> "The air is full of farewells to the dying,
> And mournings for the dead;
> The heart of Rachel for her children crying
> Will not be comforted."
> (Longfellow, " Resignation.")

Who can tell why we are cut off in the prime of usefulness?

Who knows why he is sick and weak when he wants so much to do good?

Who can understand why he is deprived of so many things he longs for—music, art, travel, books?

Who can understand why to him disaster follows disaster, loss follows loss, disappointment disappointment, from the sins of others, and not his own?

Who can understand steamboat disasters, railroad wrecks, the ravages of war, and all the cruelties and oppressions and persecutions and wrongs of every kind which give a lurid light to all history, so that it is hard to believe in the perfect goodness of God?

There are so many things of which Christ seems to say to us as he did to Peter: "What I do thou knowest not now, but thou shalt understand hereafter" (John xiii. 7.)

IN THE SECOND PLACE, how does the Voice from the Whirlwind help us?

For many years this Voice was a puzzle and a disappointment to me. When Job wanted comfort and light on his bitter sorrow, some rays from God "with healing in its wings," lo, He speaks to us of creating the world, of seas, and stars, of far away Orion and Pleiades, of snow and clouds and lightning, of leviathan and behemoth, of the wild ass and ostrich and horse and lion, of mountains and trees. What have these to do for a man whose hopes are blasted and whose body is racked with pain?

But, as a matter of fact, there was no answer possible then, better than the one God gave, by showing his infinite power, knowledge, wisdom and goodness; and saying to Man, Look at these works of mine, which you can see and touch; see my manifold wisdom, manifested in a thousand ways; see how good I am in ministering to the happiness of all living things; see how strong I am to guide the stars in their courses; see how vast I am, that none can escape my ken and care; see my knowledge that rules all nature's complicated machinery—if these things are so in that which you can understand, can you not trust me in those things which you cannot understand?   Can you not say:

> "I know not where his islands lift
>   Their fronded palms in air,
> I only know I cannot drift
>   Beyond his love and care."
>
> (Whittier, " The Eternal Goodness.")

The first time I stood at the base of the Eiffel Tower, and gazed at the elevator running up almost a thousand feet, lifted by a wire rope moved by unseen machinery, I hesitated at trusting myself to the seemingly perilous journey.   But when I learned that already thirteen millions of people had been carried without a single accident, I said to myself, that elevator has been abundantly proved and tested, I will trust myself to it.

So God bids us trust him in the unseen because he has been proved trustworthy in the seen.

Will he care for the stars and not for you?

> "The voice that rolls the stars along
>   Speaks all the promises."

Will he be wise in all physical things with a wisdom that grows greater to us the more we study his works, and not be wise in the things that pertain to immortal souls?

Will he uphold with his wisdom and power all inanimate things and not fold his children in his everlasting arms?

Will he take thought for birds and flowers, the grass of the field which to-day is and to-morrow is cast into the oven, and not care for you, oh ye of little faith? (See Matt. vi. 30.)

It is thus he comforts and strengthens our faith in the prayer his Son has taught us to pray, by sustaining the petitions with the assurance "For thine is the kingdom and the power and the glory forever."

> "And so in the wearisome journey
>   Over life's troubled sea,
> I know not the way I am going,
>   But Jesus shall pilot me."
>
> (Anon.   Quoted in Foster's
> " Cyclopedia of Poetical Illustrations," No. 3619.)

IN THE THIRD PLACE, all this from nature is imperfect without Jesus Christ, the messenger of God's love to us, the proof that he is a loving Father of all his children.

Nature alone cannot fully assure us. See the conflict finely wrought out in Tennyson's " In Memoriam " (liv–lvii.)

Nature does not seem always good. Her laws seem to work inexorably, careless of what may be the result to man, so that John Stuart Mill once wrote: "Nearly all the things which men are hanged or imprisoned for doing to one another are Nature's every day performances."

So Tennyson (in his " In Memoriam," lvi) speaks of a man

"Who trusted God was love indeed
And love Creation's final law—
Though Nature, red in tooth and claw
With ravine, shriek'd against his creed."

So Professor Huxley (in his "Lay Sermons," p. 31) uses as an illustration Retzsch's famous picture, a copy of which hangs in my study, of the young man playing chess with Satan, for his soul, the pieces on Satan's side being all the evil passions—anger, pride, sloth, sinful pleasures, selfishness, unbelief; while on the young man's side the pieces are religion, love, peace, faith, courage, and the pawns are prayers. "Substitute for the mocking fiend in the picture a calm, strong angel who is playing for love, as we say, and would rather lose than win, and I should accept it as an image of human life. . . . The chess-board is the world, the pieces are the phenomena of the universe, the rules of the game are what we call the laws of Nature. The player on the other side is hidden from us. We know that his play is always fair, just, and patient. But also we know to our cost that he never overlooks a mistake, or makes the smallest allowance for ignorance. To the man who plays well the highest stakes are paid, with the sort of overflowing generosity with which the strong shows delight in strength. And one who plays ill is checkmated without haste and without remorse."

It is in view of Nature as we thus see it that Tennyson again sings:

"I falter where I firmly trod,
And falling with my weight of cares
Upon the world's great altar-stairs
That slope through darkness up to God,

"I stretch lame hands of faith, and grope,
And gather dust and chaff, and call
To what I feel is Lord of all,
And faintly trust the larger hope."
("In Memoriam," lv.)

So Job found,
" The Deep saith, It is not in me;
And the Sea saith, It is not with me;

Destruction and Death say,
We have heard a rumor thereof with our ears."

(Job xxviii. 14, 22.)

"The Owlet Atheism
Sailing on obscene wings athwart the noon,
Drops his blue-fringed lids, and holds them close,
And hooting at the glorious Sun in heaven,
Cries out, 'Where is it?'"

(Coleridge, "Fear in Solitude.")

But all this is changed by the coming of Jesus Christ, who is the absolute proof of the love of God. "If God is for us, who is against us?"

"He that spared not his own Son, but delivered him up for us all, how shall he not also with him freely give us all things? Who shall separate us from the love of Christ? shall tribulation, or anguish, or persecution, or famine, or nakedness, or peril, or sword? Nay, in all these things we are more than conquerors through him that loved us. For I am persuaded, that neither death, nor life, nor angels, nor principalities, nor things present, nor things to come, nor powers, nor height, nor depth, nor any other creature, shall be able to separate us from the love of God, which is in Christ Jesus our Lord." (Romans viii. 31, 32, 35, 37-39.)

It is comforting to see in actual history how wicked wars have been used by God to help forward the progress of man; as the wars which brought Judah into exile, those of Alexander the Great, of Rome, of the French Revolution, of our Revolution and Civil War. The greatest mystery is to see how to the individual sufferers in these conflicts good could come.

The one thing we need to know is not the meaning of all our trials and the reason for all God does to us, but that God is our Father, that his power is limitless, his wisdom perfect, and his love is as great as his power. Our fathers may have dwelt too much in proportion on the greatness and sovereignty of God; but we are to make the proportion right, not by lessening our idea of his power, but by enlarging our idea of his love. Here we rest as a child in its mother's arms. Here we come close to God in love. It is better *not* to know all the reasons in order that we may trust and love the more.

IN THE FOURTH PLACE, when once we have seen and felt that God is a Father, a personal Friend; not Teufeldrockh's "Absentee God, sitting at the outside of the Universe, and seeing it go," but rather an ever-present God, ordaining his laws but always in them and using them; then Nature is an education, an inspiration, an unveiling of God.

Longfellow wrote of Agassiz, the great investigator of Nature:

"Here is a story book
Thy Father hath written for thee.

Come wander with me, she said,
Into regions yet untrod;
And read what is still unread
In the manuscripts of God."

Nature, without revelation, is like a great cathedral with divinely pictured windows seen from without. Nature, with revelation, is like the same cathedral seen from within.

An astronomer was converted, and was asked what he would now do with his studies. In reply he said, "I am going to heaven and will take the stars on the way." "We look through Nature up to Nature's God."

One of the most interesting articles on this general subject is Edward Everett Hale's story in which he compares Homer and David, by representing each one as singing selections from his own works: Homer from the "Iliad" and "Odyssey," and David from the Psalms.

"I gaze aloof
At the tissued roof,
Where time and space are the warp and woof,
Which the King of kings
Like a curtain flings
O'er the dreadfulness of eternal things.

"If I could see
As in truth they be,
The glories that encircle me,
I should lightly hold
This tissued fold,
With its marvellous curtain of blue and gold.

"For soon the whole,
Like a parchèd scroll,
Shall before my amazèd eyes uproll,
And without a screen,
At one burst be seen
The Presence in which I have always been."
(Whytehead.)

"Flower in the crannied wall,
I pluck you out of the crannies—
Hold you here, root and all, in my hand,
Little flower—but if I could understand
What you are, root and all, and all in all,
I should know what God and man is."
(Tennyson.)

"Earth's crammed with heaven,
And every common bush afire with God,
But only he who sees, takes off his shoes;
The rest sit round it, and pluck blackberries."
(Mrs. Browning, "Aurora Leigh," Bk. vii.)

"One impulse from a vernal wood
May teach you more of man,
Of moral evil and of good,
Than all the sages can."
(Wordsworth, "The Tables Turned.")

"Our common daily life divine
And every land a Palestine.
. . . .

The heavens are glassed in Merrimack,
What more could Jordan render back?
. . . .

This maple ridge shall Horeb be,
Yon green-banked lake our Galilee.
. . . .

Henceforth my heart shall sigh no more
For olden time and holier shore;
God's love and blessing then and there
Are now and here and everywhere."
(Whittier, "Chapel of the Hermits." See the whole poem.)

Nature is so made as a counterpart to spiritual truths that almost everything is a type or illustration, or interpreter of the spiritual world. We can find "books in the running brooks, sermons in stones, and good in everything."

"How best unfold
The secrets of another world
. . . .

By likening spiritual to corporeal forms,
As may express them best; though what if earth
Be but the shadow of heaven, and things therein
Each to other like, more than on earth is thought."
(Hugh Macmillan, "Bible Teachings in Nature," p. xviii.)

It would be a good exercise to make a list of the object lessons from nature Jesus made use of, and of their teachings; and a similar list from the Psalms and Prophets. The preaching and teaching of Jesus is full of allusions to nature, to birds, plants, seeds, sheep, mountains, floods, fields, flowers, the seasons, storms, sunshine, sunsets.

> "The flowers are the alphabet
> Of angels whereby
> They write on hills and fields
> Mysterious truths."

The light speaks to us of God, the winds of the work of the Holy Spirit; the dawn is a prophecy of the millennium; the mountains tell us of the might of faith, the fading flowers of God's loving care; the stars point to the star of Bethlehem.

Nature, being the work of the same God who gave Revelation, must be an interpreter of God and his Word.

See Mrs. Gatty's "Parables from Nature."

See Coleridge's "Hymn before Sunrise in the Vale of Chamouni," ending:

> "Tell thou the silent sky,
> And tell the stars, and tell yon rising sun,
> Earth with her thousand voices praises God."

IN THE FIFTH PLACE, the call to view nature drew Job out of himself and away from his troubles and cares. One of the first and best cures for the doubting, the sickly, the disconsolate, is to get their thoughts away from themselves, to God, to helping others, to interest in the great universe of God, and the great work of redeeming the world into the kingdom of heaven.

Note how the study of nature in science has lately furnished us with the one decisive proof that there is One God, and only one.

IN THE SIXTH PLACE, we see the double effect of this manifestation of God upon Job. (1) He learned to know God, in distinction from knowing about God. He had come close to God's heart. "Closer is he than breathing, nearer than hands and feet." (Tennyson, "The Higher Pantheism.") We all know the difference between knowing about a person, and knowing the person himself, coming into personal contact, feeling his friendship and love, entering into his feelings, and he into ours. Dr. Lyman Abbott illustrates the difference by contrasting an orphan who has heard about his father, and a child living in his father's home as a friend as well as a child.

(2) He "abhorred himself and repented in dust and ashes." He was so ignorant, how could he challenge the goodness of the Wise God, of whose vast plane for Job, in this life and the next he could have little comprehension? There is a striking passage in which a great philosopher, the famous Bishop Berkeley, describes the thought which occurred to him of the inscrutable schemes of Providence, as he saw in St. Paul's Cathedral a fly moving on one of the pillars. He says: "It requires some comprehension in the eye of an intelligent spectator to take in at one view the various parts of the building in order to observe their symmetry and design. But to the fly, whose prospect was confined to a little part of one of the stones of a single pillar, the joint beauty of the whole or the distant use of its parts, was inconspicuous. To that limited view,

the small irregularities on the surface of the hewn stone seemed to be so many deformed rocks and precipices." That fly on the pillar, of which the philosopher spoke, is the likeness of each human being as he creeps along the vast pillars which support the universe. (Dean Stanley.)

Read Edward Everett Hale's story of Hands Off, in his "Christmas in a Palace," for one of the brightest and best illustrations of trusting to God's hands all the providences that come to us, even where they seem to be against us. It represents a man in another state of existence, looking down upon Joseph as he is in the hands of the Midianites. Being an active, ingenious young man, Joseph succeeded in escaping from his captors on the first night of his captivity, and had just reached the outer limits of the camp when a yellow dog barked, awakened his captors, and Joseph was returned to his captivity. But the on-looker wanted to interfere and kill the dog before he had awakened the camp. Then Joseph would have reached home in safety, and great sorrows have been avoided. But his guardian said, "Hands Off." And to let him see the evil of his interference, took him to a world where he could try his experiment. There he killed the dog. Joseph reached home in safety, his father rejoiced, his brothers were comforted. But when the famine came, there had been no Joseph to lay up the corn. Palestine and Egypt were starved. Great numbers died, and the rest were so weakened that they were destroyed by the savage Hittites. Civilization was destroyed. Egypt was blotted out. Greece and Rome remained in a barbarous state. The whole history of the world was changed, and count-less evils came because a man in his ignorant wisdom killed a dog and saved Joseph from present trouble to his future loss.

PART V

THE CONCLUSION. PROSE.
(Chapter xli. 7-17.)

FIFTH SOLUTION: THAT EVERY GOOD MAN'S LIFE
IN THE END IS A SUCCESS. WITH GOD'S CHIL-
DREN THERE ARE NO LIFE-TRAGEDIES. THERE
ARE DRAMAS AND LYRIC SONGS AND EPICS, BUT
NO TRAGEDIES

RESEARCH QUESTIONS

(To be assigned to different members of the class at the previous session,
and for discussion in the class.)

1. In what respects was Job right, so that he could receive the divine
approval?

2. For what were the three Friends censured by God?

3. Why was a sacrifice required?

4. What was there in Job's praying for his Friends that made it a fitting
condition for his return to prosperity?

5. What were the elements in Job's reward?

6. Were the outward rewards a fitting conclusion of his career?

7. What impression would they make upon the community?

8. What is the place of material things in the rewards and fruits of
a good life?

9. What are the best rewards of virtue?

10. The descriptions of heaven as bearing on this subject.

11. Is there any difference in the teachings of the Old and the New Testa-
ments upon this subject?

12. What light does the life of Christ throw upon it?

97

THE DIVINE APPROVAL OF JOB

JOB had come to that spiritual condition that made it right and wise to restore him to health and prosperity again.

God commends Job for speaking that which was right concerning him. Not that every word was perfect, but his general position and attitude was the right one. He had kept his faith in God as just and good even when he could not see how his afflictions were right. The god against whom he had spoken was the false idea of God which his friends had presented as the true picture. Job rebelled against that picture as correct. But he was honest and loyal to the true God. He was a moral victor.

THE THREE FRIENDS were condemned because they had misrepresented God; they had been willing to be false to Job, and condemn God's child unjustly in order to defend God. They presented a false view of God's providential government. They indeed said many good and true things, but their main defence of God was not right.

A SACRIFICE was necessary as expressing the need of atonement for sin, and as a sign of their repentance.

JOB'S CAPTIVITY WAS TURNED when he prayed for his Friends. This showed (1) that he had forgiven them for all the hard words they had spoken about him, and the bitter burden they had added to his calamity; and (2) had gone out of himself in his interest for others.

Both these were essential conditions of his restoration. He that will not forgive cannot be forgiven. And he that is self-centred would make a bad use of his relief from trouble.

Thus Job was prepared for his new life, higher, nobler, richer than even his good life before his trial.

THE FINAL OUTCOME

THE FACTS.—The Epilogue states the final outcome of his trial so far as it was visible, "a living epistle known and read of all men."

1. **His friends were restored.** They sympathized with him, and brought him aid to restore his lost fortunes: a piece of silver—an uncoined piece of unknown value—and a ring of gold, either an ornament, or more probably one of the rings which the Egyptians used for money.

2. **His property became double** that which he had possessed before his affliction.

3. **He had the delight of children**—seven sons and three daughters, whose names signified a Dove, Fragrant Cinnamon, and Cornucopia, a horn of plenty, expressing their attractive characters combined with rare beauty. He lived a long life, saw his descendants to the fourth generation. His life was

" Rich in experience that angels might covet,
Rich in a faith that had grown with the years."

And Wordsworth's wish for his friend,[1]

"An old age serene and bright,
And lovely as a Lapland night,
Shall lead thee to thy grave,"

was fulfilled in Job.

His sunset colors were more radiant than the noontide sun could give. They were like the gates of Paradise overarched with the rainbow of hope. The Greek Garden of the Hesperides was in the west.

One thinks of Bunyan's Christian passing through the dark river with bands of welcoming angels waiting to greet him on the other side.

THIS BEAUTIFUL PICTURE of Job's later life, the outcome of his sufferings, has been severely criticised as an unworthy ending of the poem, a descent from the climax of the drama, and therefore written by another hand than that of the great poet.

But to my mind this ending is an essential element of the movement of the poem. It is the natural and proper climax of Job's life; and all feelings of its unworthiness arise from a misinterpretation of its significance.

"When the Devil asked with a sneer, 'Doth Job fear God for nought?' he was looking at the matter only from the Devil's standpoint—that of selfishness. But it was true, in a way, that the Devil and those who serve him cannot understand that Job did *not* fear God for nought, nor has any one ever served and feared God for nought. The returns from God's service are bigger and better than all that any competing employer has to offer."

First. We must keep clearly in mind the distinction between the rewarding results which follow and grow out of a right course of action and wages which are sought and received for performing that action. The promise is that to those who seek first the kingdom of God and his righteousness "all these things shall be added," and the whole history of Christian civilization is an illustration and confirmation. But those who seek first, chiefly, "all these things," do not belong to the Kingdom of God. What they get they get as wages, as gifts to draw them to better things, not as fruits, and they fail of the best. The two characters are entirely different. One will do right whatever the consequences; the other is merely seeking something to his own advantage.

The results do not follow in each individual case immediately, or the temptation would be too great to forget the right doing in the presence of the reward. But as a whole, to the community, they do follow.

Professor Münsterberg, in "The Americans," states the case clearly: "The American merchant works for money in exactly the sense that a great painter works for money; the high price which is paid for his picture is a very welcome indication of the general appreciation of his art; but he would never get this appreciation if he were working for the money instead of his artistic ideals." (P. 238.)

"In the United States wealth has great significance only because it is felt to measure the individual's successful initiative. . . . He wishes in this way to express the fact that he has passed life's examinations well, that he has been enterprising, and has won the respect of those around him." (P. 240.)

The Outlook for July 29, 1905, in an article on " Teachers' Salaries," expresses the same distinction in this way:

"It is not desirable that either the Church or the State should bid against industrial enterprises—and for a very simple reason. A man may be a successful leader of industry who measures its success by the pecuniary reward it gives to him; but no man can be a successful soldier, or statesman, or teacher, or preacher who adopts any such standard. No one wishes to see such pecuniary rewards offered by the civil service, the school, or the Church as will entice into it men chiefly by hope of pecuniary reward. No one supposes that Henry Ward Beecher ought to have received as preacher and lecturer an income five times as great as he did receive, because as a jury lawyer he would easily have made that amount; no one wishes to see the Nation paying to Mr. Root as Secretary of State an income approximating that which he surrendered when he became Secretary of State. But just because the teacher, the preacher, and the publicist should be enabled to dismiss financial considerations and devote themselves wholly to the service to which the public calls them, the public should furnish an income on which they can live with comfort and dignity."

President Roosevelt in a late address made the same distinction.

Now the reward of Job was of the better and nobler kind. It was the right and noble fruit of an entirely disinterested course of life which sought the highest things without looking for reward.

Second. The outward prosperity which came to Job after his victory in his great trial was the symbol and visible expression of the spiritual results, the nobler character, the larger love, the firmer faith, which were the real rewards.

If Job had been left a poor, lonely, broken down old man, to wear out his life in a weary struggle with want, though he became a saint as holy as the seraphim the result of his trial and of the teaching would have been obscured, both to his neighbors and to the world ever since.

Heaven with all its outward glories, and not hell, is the fitting environment for the eternal abode of those who have the heavenly spirit and life. If one seeks merely a heavenly place—the golden streets, the river of peace flowing among fruit trees, the emerald bow about the throne, the jewelled walls and gates of pearl—he is not seeking heaven, nor on the way to heaven, nor can he get there by that road.

"Who seeks for heaven alone to save his soul
May keep the path, but will not reach the goal.
While he who walks in love may wander far,
Yet God will bring him where the blessed are."
(Anon.)

Whoever really seeks heaven seeks after the heavenly character, the heavenly life; seeks to live according to the beatitudes, the life of love, the fruits of the spirit, the life of doing good, the life which Jesus lived, all the things which make heaven what it is. The outward glories are the expression and fitting environment of the heavenly spirit. That is the real meaning of our songs of heaven, our "glory songs." Says Dr. Robert E. Speer:

"It would be as sensible to tell a mariner to stop thinking about his port, and just steer any way, only so he went straight for the moment, as to bid us stop living with reference to the heaven we are bound for."

Third. The need of this outward expression and fitting environment is seen on every hand as we would persuade men to live the religious life. Men are repelled by what they regard the gloominess of the Christian life. A late writer voices his antipathy to what he pictures as the Puritan forefathers' heaven, "a place of ages of psalm-singing, of harp-playing, of praise." The repellent dulness of the conception of goodness by not a few is pictured by the London preacher's story of the little girl who asked her father if he did not think that when she got to heaven, if she was real good and played with the angels all the morning, the Lord would let her have a little devil to play with in the afternoon. So, too, Rasselas, wishing to escape from the Happy Valley; and Professor James's first experience of Chautauqua, as given in his recent book, "Talks to Teachers on Psychology," pp. 268–75.

The heathen nations are willing to listen with greater interest to appeals from Christian nations because they see what Christianity has done for them.

Suppose we make two maps of the world, on the plan furnished by the United States census, to show the degree in which ignorance, certain diseases, and many other things prevail, by means of lighter and darker shades. On one map we will note the countries where the purest Christianity prevails, by white. A darker shade will mark the more imperfect forms, and then let the shades grow darker and darker through Mohammedanism and the various forms of heathenism, till we come to the blackness of the lowest fetichism.

Then, with entire independence, make a similar map of the moral and intellectual condition of men. Where there is the most manhood, the noblest womanhood, the highest morality, the most of all that elevates the people, and brings the greatest happiness, these put in white, darken the shades as these things grow less, till we come to the blackness of the lowest savagery.

Bring the two maps together and they will exactly coincide. Where there is the most Christianity there will be the most of all that is good for man.

It is inconceivable that the good God should make a world the laws of which were not beautiful and beneficent to all who obey them. And this is well, because the material blessings which flow from obedience become the means and instruments for the service of God and man. They help to hasten "the Good Time Coming."

Fourth. Both the Old Testament and the New teach this doctrine of the final outcome of right character.

The Old Testament is full of it. See Deuteronomy and the Prophets and the Wisdom Literature.

And it is not a worn-out dogma of the dead Past. With larger emphasis on the spiritual and eternal rewards Christ teaches the same truth and makes the same promises. Look at his list of seven rewards he promises to those who overcome. (Rev. ii, iii.)

Heaven, a holy but also a beautiful heaven, is placed at the end of the Bible as the final consummation.

The same is true of the ideal man, Jesus Christ himself, "who for the joy that was set before him endured the cross, despising the shame, and is set down at the right hand of the throne of God." (Heb. xii. 2.)

We are apt to look at the cross as the ultimate end of Jesus, or to dwell on it so much that we forget his ascension, his glorious appearance as revealed in Revelation, as King of Kings, and Lord of Lords, reigning in unspeakable glory. All this is absolutely unselfish and therefore divine.

Fifth. Let us look at the real rewards which crowned Job's victory in his long trial.

(1) He received a great and blessed development of character. He entered the higher ranges and visions of goodness and faith and love. His eyes were opened like those of Elisha's servant to see truths and enjoy experiences which never entered even his dreams before. His spiritual experience was like Jacob's ladder by which he climbed nearer to heaven and to God.

> "The soul's dark cottage, battered and decayed,
> Lets in new light through chinks that time has made."
> (Edmund Waller, "Verses upon his Divine Poesy.")

The greatest reward of goodness is more goodness, of love is more love, of faith is a fuller trust.

> "To each of us all there will come an hour
> When the tree of life shall burst into flower,
> And rain at our feet a glorious dower
> Of something greater than ever we knew."

Some one has said: "It is true that troubles never come singly, but in a better sense than is usually meant by that phrase. No consignment of trouble is ever sent to us by itself. By the same messenger there comes a consignment of special strength to bear that trouble—and the strength-package is always a little larger than the trouble-package." But more than strength come discipline, growth, larger vision, nearness to God, power to help others, purer living, deeper thinking—all come with trouble, if we will receive them.

Compare Milton's experience after his blindness came, as interpreted by Elizabeth Lloyd:

"O Merciful One! Thy glorious face
    Is leaning toward me, and its holy light
Shines in upon my lonely dwelling-place
    And there is no night.

"Oh, I seem to stand
    Trembling where foot of mortal ne'er hath been,
Wrapped in the radiance of thy sinless land
    Which eye hath never seen.

"Visions come and go,
    Shapes of resplendent beauty round me throng,
From angel lips I seem to hear the flow
    Of soft and holy song.

"It is nothing now—
    When heaven is ripening on my sightless eyes
When airs from Paradise refresh my brow—
    That earth in darkness lies.

"In a purer clime
    My being fills with rapture; waves of thought
Roll in upon my spirit, strains sublime
    Break over me unsought."

(2) Job received such prosperity as expressed God's approval and could be seen and recognized by men, a symbol for them of his inner experience.

(3) Job received in his soul increased power of helpfulness and usefulness. As Paul says to the Corinthians: "The God of all comfort . . . comforteth us in all our affliction, that we may be able to comfort them that are in any affliction, through the comfort wherewith we ourselves are comforted of God." (2 Cor. i. 4.)

And more than this, his increased prosperity under this new inspiration increased his power of helping others. The adding of 7000 sheep to his previous 7000 added nothing whatever to his personal enjoyment, any more than another million added to the millionaire's dollars increases his happiness. But the doubling of his property gave additional power of usefulness; put a better instrument for doing good into his hands. That is what the right character can do with all the material things which so often tempt us to evil. God does not ask us to exterminate them, but to transform them into instruments of blessing, as the inner light in Goethe's "Tale of Tales" transformed the rude log hut of the fisherman into an exquisitely wrought temple of solid silver.

Job lives in the lives of those he has comforted, and has a part in the betterment of millions of lives all down the ages.

(4) Job's reward was perfected in eternal life. In the Septuagint version, made some two centuries before Christ, "we find a clause added that strikes another key, hints that we have before us only the first scenes in a drama not yet played out, only the first stages of the endless life.—'And it is written that he will rise again with those whom the Lord raiseth up.' "

> "And when these earthly years are past and gone,
> Temptation's battle fought, the victory won,
> From heaven shall gently come this message down,
> They that have borne the cross shall wear a crown
> Never to fade."

> "If thou wilt be a hero, and wilt strive
> To help thy fellow and exalt thyself,
> Thy feet, at last, shall stand on jasper floors;
> Thy heart, at last, shall seem a thousand hearts—
> Each single heart with myriad raptures filled—
> While thou shalt sit with princes and with kings,
> Rich in the jewel of a ransomed soul."

A German writer illustrates the greatness of our salvation after this manner: A gentleman, after the most exemplary life, died. The gate of heaven was opened, and he was welcomed as an heir of glory. One of the glorious ones was commissioned to be his conductor and teacher. First he took him to a point where he could see the most fearful representation of sin, in its fruits of misery. The objects of horror made him shudder. Then his guide bade him look farther and farther down in the dismal vault, and he saw the most hideous and terrible of beings, the fruit of sin. "*That*," said his guide, "*is what in the ages of eternity you would have been had you gone on in sin.*" His guide next took him to a point from which could be seen the glories of the redeemed. He saw rank after rank of angels, seraphim, and cherubim, dwelling in ineffable glory. He bade him look beyond these; and in the far distance he beheld a being transcendently more radiant and glorious, around whom floated the soft music of unspeakable sweetness and joy. "*That*," said the guide, "*is yourself many ages hence.* Behold the glory and bliss to which the salvation of Jesus will bring you."

See the hymn "For all the saints who from their labors rest."

See Archbishop Trench's poem beginning "I say to thee, do thou repeat," and ending, "That this *is* blessing, this *is* life."

Dr. Samuel Cox closes his noble book on Job with these words:

"Whoever has learned to see in suffering a proof of God's love, and beyond the darkness of death a land of light, in which all wrongs shall be redressed, and all virtue meet its due reward—a land, in fine, in which the varied discipline of this world shall issue in a life conformed to its fair and high ideal, and cherished by all happy and auspicious conditions—he has a solution of the great Problem in which he may rest and rejoice."

We may well sum up the impressions the book has left upon us in the ascription which Blake has engraved above the final plate of his noble "Inventions of Job."

"Great and Marvellous are Thy Works, Lord God Almighty;
Just and True are Thy Ways, O Thou King of Saints."

"Ye have heard of the Patience of Job, and have seen the end of the Lord, how that the Lord is full of pity and merciful." (James v. 1.)

INDEXES

I

GENERAL INDEX

II

REFERENCES TO LITERATURE